Counsels o[·]
for Christian Mothers

BY

THE VERY REVEREND P. LEJEUNE

Honorary Canon of the Cathedral of Reims
Archpriest of Charleville

TRANSLATED WITH THE
AUTHOR'S PERMISSION

BY

FRANCIS A. RYAN

NIHIL OBSTAT

Sti. Ludovici, die 21. Oct. 1913

> *F. G. Holweck,*
> *Censor Librorum*

IMPRIMATUR

Sti. Ludovici, die 21. Oct. 1913

> ✠ *Joannes J. Glennon,*
> *Archiepiscopus*
> *Sti. Ludovici*

CONTENTS

PART ONE

CONTENTS

CONTENTS

PART FIRST

THE END—OBSTACLES

COUNSELS OF PERFECTION

CHAPTER I

TRUE AND FALSE DEVOTION

My daughters, you all aspire to perfection. But what is your idea of perfection? Do you not often use this word in a vague and even false sense? It trips so lightly into your conversation that each one prides herself on having a very clear conception of it. I am positive, however, that if I were to ask you to define this word, the response would be a confusion of tongues.

Perfection is frequently attributed to persons who assume strained attitudes and an affected bearing. Now this notion of perfection is erroneous; for these strained attitudes and this affectation, far from constituting true perfection, are but counterfeits of it.

For many, perfection consists in an invariable series of prayers. They consider it a crime to fail to make the sign of the cross, to omit one of the multiple invocations to some saint in Paradise, or to cut short a novena or some other pious practice. The laws of justice, the injunctions of charity, the rules of prudence, humility and modesty are elements of perfection to which these people give not the slightest concern. This type of devotees is by no means new. It flourished even in the days of our Saviour. You may recall to mind the Pharisees whom Jesus reproached for straining the gnat, and swallowing the camel.

The author of the *Imitation* severely rebukes those who center all their devotion on books, images, and exterior signs and symbols. I am not sure that some of you are not given to this whimsical and purely exterior piety. Some of you perhaps permit your interior life to lie fallow, because you have in your rooms an altar of the Blessed Virgin or the Sacred Heart arranged with taste, and adorned with the fairest flowers of the season . . . Let us smile and pass on.

Here is another error. We find it among those honest but short-sighted people who insist upon viewing the spiritual life from one side only. This error lies in identifying perfection with macerations and corporeal penances. According to this view, he alone reaches the highest degree of perfection who can best submit to the blows of discipline, or to long-continued fasts. Now I have often read that sanctity adapts itself admirably to ordinary life, and does not at all entail the extraordinary and terrifying attendance of corporeal penances.

If this be our idea of perfection, then our idea is not correct.

Let us read a passage from St. Francis de Sales, in which he describes with his usual grace all the counterfeits of perfection.

"You must first know what the virtue of devotion is; for since there is but one true devotion, and many which are false and deceitful, if you cannot distinguish that which is true, you may easily deceive yourself in following some fantastical and superstitious devotion.

"As Aurelius painted all the faces of his pictures to the resemblance of the woman he loved, so every one paints devotion according to his own passion and fancy. He that is addicted to fasting thinks himself very devout if he fasts, though his heart be at the same time filled with rancor, and scrupling to moisten his tongue with wine, or even with water, through sobriety, he makes no difficulty to drink deep of his neighbor's blood, as it were, by detraction and calumny. Another considers himself devout because he recites daily a multitude of prayers, though immediately afterwards he utters the most disagreeable, arrogant, and injurious words amongst his domestics and neighbors. Another cheerfully draws money out of his purse to relieve the poor, but cannot draw meekness out of his heart to forgive his enemies. Another readily forgives his enemies, but never satisfies his creditors except by constraint.

These may be esteemed devout by some, but in reality, they are by no means so.

"When Saul's servants sought David in his house, Michol, laying a statue in his bed, and covering it with his clothes, made them believe it was David himself; thus many persons, by covering themselves with certain external actions make the world believe that they are truly devout, whereas they are in reality nothing but statues and phantoms of devotion."

*

* *

Having pointed out the counterfeits of perfection, I must now proceed to give a precise definition of it. But you must remember that it is exceedingly difficult to shape a definition which can be applied to all natures without exception. The saints, judging them on the surface, differ vastly in their ideas of perfection. The severe St. Jerome, for example, seems to have a very remote relation to the sweet St. Francis de Sales. St. Aloysius of Gonzaga and St. Stanislaus—delicate flowers that expanded in the peace and regularity of the religious life

—bear but little resemblance to St. Francis Xavier, who, preceding the most daring explorers, traversed the world to win kingdoms for Jesus Christ.

If I study the writings of the saints, if I recall the words that fell from their lips, and strive from these to form an idea of true perfection, I am again plunged into perplexity. I hear St. Francis of Assisi preaching: ''Be ye poor; this is perfection.'' I hear St. Vincent de Paul repeating: ''Be ye charitable; this is perfection.'' I hear the Abbé de Rancey, the austere reformer of the Trappists, saying: ''Be ye mortified; this is perfection.''

So I might heap up citation upon citation, but these will suffice to show how difficult it is to arrive at a formula for perfection which will fit all the saints, determine the common trait which permits us to classify them all under one head, and enables us to say of each one, ''Here is a saint.''

*

*   *

My daughters, I trust that the definition of

perfection which I shall give, will sink deeply into your hearts. *Perfection is accomplishing the will of God in a constant and generous fashion.* That person, then, is perfect who does at every instant what God wishes. Ask her at any moment what she is doing, and she will always respond: "That which God wishes." If a response other than that be obtained from her, for example: "I am doing what pleases myself, or some other creature," then you have the right to say: "This person is not perfect."

Do you ask for an example of a perfect woman? I shall give it to you from the heavenly hierarchy, by recalling the life of Mary, who, in the matter of perfection, is the nearest approach to God. She it is whom I charge to prove my thesis in such a way that you will be clearly persuaded that sanctity does not at all consist in splendor or magnificence or the glitter of exterior things, but rather in an interior principle which animates the most ordinary actions, and communicates to them an almost inestimable value.

Consider for a moment the life of Mary. What do you find rare or extraordinary in that life? It was the life of a plain Judean woman in the century of Augustus. It was spent in the monotony of the most commonplace occupations. We see Mary as a child growing up pious and pure under her mother's care. We see her as a young maiden, espousing a workman. We see her as a mother watching over her slumbering Infant. We see her as a housewife preparing food for the husband and the Son returning from their labors. Yet this woman is holy, incomparably holier than all the saints taken together; holy with a holiness before which all other holiness pales, as the light of the stars pales when the sun rises above the horizon. I challenge any one to find another explanation of Mary's sanctity than this: Mary was accomplishing the will of God at every moment of her life, and the perfect love with which she accomplished that will, constituted the measure of her sanctity.

Moreover, this rule can be applied to all the saints.

Do not invoke the name of Francis Xavier, because he won kingdoms for Jesus Christ. Do not invoke the name of St. Vincent de Paul, because he gathered all the wretched under the folds of his robe. Do not invoke the name of St. John Baptist de La Salle, because he permitted his love for children to develop into heroism. If St. Francis had baptised the Japanese and the Indians without the command of God, he would not be holy. If St. Vincent de Paul had sheltered all the suffering under his robe, without the command of God, he would not be holy. If St. John Baptist de La Salle had, without divine command, sold his goods and renounced all dignities, in order to become master of a school, he would not be holy. It was the will of God realized by them, and accomplished in them, that made these men saints.

Thus understood, perfection no longer appears to us as the privilege of the few. There are no professions to which it is allied to the exclusion of other professions. There are no countries to which it adapts itself to the exclusion of other countries. It is for all times, for all countries, and for all states and professions. Whatever may be your station in life, whether you were born of poor parents, like our Saviour, or whether you spring from a family where ease and even opulence reigns, it matters little. Remember that perfection can and ought to harmonize with every state and condition.

The outline of perfection which I have sketched in this chapter does not originate with me. I have taken it from the words of the Saviour, who, far from designating certain individuals says to us all: "Be ye perfect."

Let me recall to your minds that beautiful prayer which a holy princess, Mme. Elizabeth, daughter of a king, and sister of Louis XVI, made each morning of her life; and I charge you to repeat it every day, if not verbatim, at least in its general sense: "My God, what will happen to me to-day, I do not know; but I do know that nothing will happen to me which Thou hast not foreseen and ordained for my greater good. I accept, then, Thy thrice holy will; I submit myself to it, and desire to delight in it despite all the revolts of my reason, and the repugnances of my nature."

CHAPTER II

WHAT is the state of my soul? What place do I occupy, with regard to God, in the great family of Christian souls? These, my daughters, are questions to which you must not be indifferent. In order to furnish you with the elements of a response to these questions, I intend to draw up a catalogue of souls which will enable you to determine to what category you belong. My purpose, I must avow, is not solely to satisfy your curiosity. When you know just where your place is in this catalogue you should aspire to a higher degree of excellence in the hierarchy of souls. It is my purpose to guide you in your upward march, to point out the halting-places along the way, and to indicate the means by which you can arrive most quickly and most surely at the coveted goal.

A preliminary observation: The catalogue that I shall draw up is not at all concerned with those who live in the state of habitual mortal sin. I write for those earnest Christians who, to say the least, never commit a grave fault. If some one among my readers should be so unfortunate as to live continually at enmity with God, this poor soul would be an object to weep over and to pray for, but not to delay upon.

What principle is to guide us in our classification of souls? Which one of our faculties will instruct us as to the state of our souls, and authorize us to decide, without fear of error, whether this or that soul is ill or well? Let us interrogate successively our three chief faculties: the sensibility, the intelligence, and the will.

Will the sensibility instruct us infallibly as to the state of a soul? No! The sensibility is a faculty which deceives us even in the ordinary affairs of life, and which, in our relations with God, baffles all our calculations, and evades all our previsions. For example, to-day you feel that your affection for some person you love is much less lively than yesterday, and you are at a loss to account for this. You have done nothing which, to your knowledge, might produce this effect. So in the affairs of piety you will experience vacillations yet more pronounced, and not less inexplicable. To-day, full of ardor in prayer, you open your soul before God without the least effort, and experience a deep feeling of love for Him. To-morrow, your prayers seem but empty words which your sensibility disavows. Evidently your sensibility has undergone a change. But has the state of your soul changed? Not at all! In the eyes of God you are the same as you were yesterday, despite your seeming lukewarmness.

It is not to the sensibility, then, that we must have recourse when we wish to determine our place in the catalogue of souls. To take this faculty for our guide would be to expose ourselves to innumerable disappointments. We should be great saints at times when our hearts beat more lively in prayer than is customary with us; but we should be the worst miscreants when we prayed without relish and happiness.

Are you not aware, my daughters, that the majority of the saints had to endure this absence of sensible relish, and these vacillations of the sensibility, which, in their relations with God, brought them agony and torture rather than joy? We may well believe them when they tell us that in prayer they were "beasts of burden before God." But was their prayer less meritorious and efficacious because it was not accompanied by sensible joy? The sensibility, then, is a faculty which we cannot be too distrustful of when we desire to render to ourselves an account of our standing with God.

*

* *

Is the intelligence our infallible guide? Does the vigor of our spiritual life depend upon this faculty? It would, if to know good were to do good. But how frequently we find those of enlightened intelligence satisfied to let their morality consist mainly in desire! It is so seldom that we love God in the measure in which we know Him. It is not at all impossible to have a consummate knowledge of religion and the spiritual life, to be a light for others, and yet resemble the guide-post which points the way, but itself remains immovable.

Moreover, would it be just for our spiritual vitality to be in proportion to the various lights which God gives us? There are some on whom God has bestowed light sparingly; there are others on whom He has shed it abundantly. But what is light? It is but the means of knowing good. Thus each one is held to do good in the measure in which she comprehends it. Abundance of light, then, is a gift for which we shall be judged more severely by God; and if we bring to His tribunal an intelligence rich in light, and a life poor in merits, we may well be fearful.

It is not to the intelligence you must look, therefore, in order to ascertain the state of your spiritual life.

There remains, now, the will. How is your will disposed towards God? Is your will united to the will of God? Do you wish what God wishes, the least important things as well as the most essential? Do you make some reserve, yielding to the divine will on one point, and opposing it on another? These, my daughters, are questions the import of which you will at once appreciate; questions which are of capital significance for you. It is indeed true that the will is the important faculty in the spiritual man. Hence it is that Catholic theology styles the sinful soul, "a will turned away from God," and the fervent soul, "a will which adheres to God."

Moreover, recall the definition of perfection which we have given in the preceding chapter: *Perfection consists in accomplishing the will of God in a constant and generous fashion.* Thus it follows that we withdraw from or approach perfection according as we shun the divine will, or adhere more generously to it.

We have at hand, then, the solution of our problem: the will must teach us the state of the soul. What is the attitude of my will relative to God? When I have responded to this question, I know what the state of my soul is; I can classify my soul; I can tell to what category it belongs.

The principle which we have just laid down will permit a classification of souls which I trust will be satisfactory to my readers.

1. Those whose souls are lukewarm, and who accept only the struggle against mortal sin.

2. Those whose souls are fervent, and who not only struggle against venial sin, but also undertake to reform themselves.

3. Those whose souls are very fervent, and who are habitually disposed to refuse God nothing.

The first of these three categories calls for some remarks. The signs of lukewarmness are indicated by the general rules which I have laid down. I have found them well drawn out in a fine passage taken from one of the works of Père Jennesseaux on the spiritual exercises of St. Ignatius:

Signs of lukewarmness: To have little or no regard for venial sin, and to fear only mortal sin; to perform one's spiritual exercises out of a spirit of routine or human respect, with disgust and with negligence reflected upon and consented to; to pray habitually without attention; to confess one's faults lightly, without the serious resolution of avoiding them; to communicate without devotion, by not striving to obtain it; to perform one's daily actions without the proper intention, without order or method; to be given over to exterior things; to be rarely present to one's self, and yet more rarely to have God present; to renounce the exercise of great virtues, even those whose practice is suited to one's state or profession; to be content with a state of mediocrity; to shun the company of those who work with ardor for their perfection; to seek the company of those who are more dissipated, less fervent and less regular; to form an erroneous conscience, the cause of which superiors and directors often attribute to lack of good judgment; to employ false principles to silence remorse; to nourish, despite the frequent use of the sacraments, interior aversions, jealousies, movements of pride, and particular and dangerous affections; to encourage a spirit of harshness, insubordination and cavilling, which manifests itself in offensive and contentious words; to entertain continually a secret self-love, which, mingling in all one's actions, corrupts and infects them with its virus; lastly, to shirk whatever entails labor and self-abnegation, and to seek rather for comforts, futile consolations, and ease.

From this simple statement, you can tell to what category you belong. After having read the chapters that will follow, you will be yet more capable of judging, will better understand how one can pass from one of these states into the other.

Very happy should I be if this study would stimulate those among you who are lukewarm to march with a resolute step to the conquest of fervor, and should inspire those already fervent, with the desire to mount higher and still higher in fervor and love.

CHAPTER III

My daughters, permit me to denounce, under the name of Naturalism, a wide-spread evil of our day, an evil that infects the soul in various ways. Surely you are not ignorant of the vast difference between the soul of the Christian and the soul of the Pagan. The will and intelligence of the Christian have received a new life, superadded to that of nature, and called for that reason the supernatural life.

Analyze the intelligence of the Christian, and you will see that it is formed and fashioned in an entirely different way than the intelligence of the Pagan. You will find there certain truths which reason itself could not have discovered, and a unity of conviction and judgment that has not sprung from natural causes.

Apply yourselves with the same earnestness to the study of the Christian's will: you will obtain the same results. You will behold this will loving persons and things to which the will of the Pagan is indifferent. For example, you will see the supernatural man regarding the Sacred Host with love, and the natural man casting only a vacant glance upon it.

The soul of the Christian is cast in a supernatural mould. The supernatural life is its foundation. Hence the Supernatural ought to rule our thoughts, and be the principal inspiration of all our actions.

Now there are certain Christians who live continuously in the state of grace, and observe the chief precepts of religion, but who, in the ordinary course of their lives, do not differ notably from Pagans. In their mode of appreciating persons and things, they manifest sentiments which have nothing of the supernatural in them. Their souls have remained partly pagan. We are right then in characterizing by the name of *naturalism,* the evil with which they are tainted.

Although their souls have received a new life,

these persons think, feel and act, as if they were yet in the life of nature.

My daughters, some of you may be forced to confess that your souls are yet pagan-like. Perhaps a truly Christian education has been denied you, and the atmosphere of religious indifference, in which you have lived, has left its stamp upon you. Perhaps you have permitted the fire of that Christian life, which burned so brightly in your earlier years, to die out. Occasionally now you sit down before the fire-grate of that life, and stir up the smouldering embers.

*

* *

Whatever may have been the origin of this semi-paganism in these people of whom I write, they all have this one trait in common: a cold indifference towards Jesus Christ. This is a natural sequence; for, since Jesus is the Author and Source of our supernatural life, it is from Him and through Him that it comes to us. Why should we be astonished, then, that a soul tainted by naturalism is indifferent towards Jesus Christ?

How often have I heard people deploring their inability to approach near to Jesus, and expressing their envy of those who find, in the love of the Master, a food for the heart, and a consolation in the hours of trial. The words and examples of Jesus have made no impression on these people. His Sacred Person, so real for many others, is to them a mere abstraction. In one word Jesus is not a real being for them.

What do those pages of the Gospel, read so assiduously by the devout, mean to them? Nothing! Their hearts do not vibrate at the recital of all that Jesus has done for them in His mortal life. What says the Tabernacle to them? Hardly anything! Their faith is so weak, so little awakened! But what terror would seize them if the mask of indifference were torn off; if the God whom they carry in them after Communion, should suddenly reveal Himself as He really is, so good, so tender, so compassionate, all glorious and resplendent with light. How confounded and humiliated they would be at their want of appreciation for Christ's great majesty. How profoundly would they reproach themselves for having been indifferent to such love, and for returning nothing for it save a distracted thanks.

Now these honest Pagans, whom I am describing, are wont to despair of themselves, and to imagine that the Christian sense is wanting in them, just as certain persons are wanting in appreciation for music and poetry. Consequently, they are led to believe that whatever they do, this Christian sense will never awaken in them. I rejoice to be able to fill them with hope, and to assure them that they possess this treasure, though it lies buried under a debris of negligence, venial faults and unchristian habits. Since they are in the state of grace, they have a true love of Jesus in the depths of their souls: a very passive love, it is true, but a love that is real, nevertheless. To awaken this love, and to make it active, is within the reach of every one. The important thing is to proceed with method, and to submit with docility to the treatment which we shall soon advise.

There is very little to despair of in these people, because they often possess precious natural qualities. Indeed many of them are capable of great things. They perhaps will never go out of their way to adopt a religious practice which is not commanded, or to work with a view to their own personal sanctification; but the day wherein they will have recognized Jesus, the day wherein they will have comprehended the immense love of Jesus, the day wherein Jesus will have become a real being for them, on that day all the energy that they have wasted on creatures, will find its place in the supernatural life, and bloom into Christian virtues.

Oh! how often have such people, after shaking off their semi-paganism, accomplished great things in the spiritual life!

CHAPTER IV

THE VALUE OF TIME

WHAT good reasons we have for valuing our time, and making good use of it! The few years which God gives us to live, enclosed as they are between the centuries that are gone and those that are to come, are indeed a trifle compared with eternity. Regarded from this standpoint, our life resembles that of those insects called, I believe, Ephemera. They are born in the morning, and in the evening they have ceased to exist. Better yet, our life resembles a wave, raised up by the wind on the bosom of the sea, that scintillates an instant under the rays of the sun, and then falls back and is no more. Or again it is like to those flashes of lightning which, on a stormy night, dazzle the eye for a moment, and then disappear without leaving a trace of their existence. And this inconceivable rapidity, this nothingness of human life condemns at once all the ambitions and desires which attach us to the earth. What folly, then, when we consider the brevity of life, to dream of cutting a great figure here below, to yearn for the admiration of the world, and to attach our hearts to those earthly goods from which we shall be so brutally separated on the morrow.

All this is truth itself! These thoughts are truly Christian thoughts! The pleasures of life could not seduce the holy men who sounded the vanity of those earthly attractions which captivate the worldling.

But so far, we have considered only one side of the question. Though life is brief, it is, at the same time, a treasure, the most precious of all treasures.

Americans have an adage which well expresses their principal preoccupation: "Time," they say, "is money." Let us adopt this adage, but let us Christianize it, and say: "Time is the money with which we can purchase eternity." Yes, it is during our fleeting existence here that our eternal destiny must be decided. It is on the employment of these few days which we have to live, that our eternal lot depends.

Hence, how important it is for us to realize the value of time, and use it to advantage. Each one of the instants of which it is composed, if we employ them according to the will of God, is the small coin with which we can purchase a superior degree of glory in Heaven. Yes, the present moment, which to all appearance is such a trifle, and which to mind is but the lightning flash, this moment, if I utilize it according to the designs of God, will give me a more intimate possession of God, and a more entrancing communion with Him for all eternity.

Why be astonished then that the Holy Spirit places so much insistence on the good employment of our time! I should never end were I to repeat to you all the passages of Holy Writ in which we are exhorted not to lose a moment of our time. I shall confine myself to these short extracts: "Son, observe the time, and fly from evil." (Ecclesiasticus iv, 23.) "Therefore, whilst we have time, let us do good." (Gal. vi, 10.)

Need we be astonished at the fidelity with which the Saints have put their maxims into practice? I defy any one to find even one of them who did not employ his time to the best advantage. Are not holiness and the proper employment of time intimately related then? A saint who would have trifled with time, who would have squandered it, or thrown it to the winds of vanity or frivolity, would be one whom we might well ridicule, and you yourselves would politely invite him to descend from a pedestal to which he had no right. St. Francis Borgia, when he was yet in the world, thus answered those who sought to have him devote a part of his time to the vanities of social life: "Let me alone, for I prefer to pass for a common person, rather than lose my time." St. Alphonsus bound himself by a vow never to lose a moment of time, and it is this vow that accounts for the wonderful works of this saint; it was this vow that enabled him to accomplish by word and example a sum of work that appears to us beyond the power of man.

Others there are, my daughters, who appreciate the value of time—but alas; too late. These people are at this moment in Hell. What would they not give could they have but one hour in which to do penance! Listen to the expression of their regret: "I had ample time, when I was on the earth, to save my soul, and prepare for myself a place in Heaven; but I foolishly squandered it. I employed it in the pursuit of vain phantoms which men call pleasure, riches, and honors. These, all these in turn were mine; but they left me, when perchance I had attained them, naught save emptiness, deception, and chagrin. While on earth I was ignorant of true happiness, and behold I shall be ignorant of it throughout all eternity. Oh! for one moment of that time which I have so foolishly squandered." And lo! like to a mocking echo, the voice of the Demon responds: "Too late! too late! For you time is no more. You have lavished your time on all the vanities with which I have tempted you. Attain these, I said, and you will be happy. Fool! Well may you weep over your folly."

My daughters, if the Elect in Heaven could experience regret, it would be a regret for the loss of time; and if they could form a desire, that desire would be for a few moments of time. A pious Benedictine, appearing after his death to one of his companions, said to him, that he was, indeed, perfectly happy, but that if he were able to desire anything, it would be to return to earth so that he might make a better use of his time, and thus secure a higher degree of glory in Heaven.

Let us consider now, my daughters, the various ways in which we are losing time: by remaining inactive, by permitting ourselves to be idle, and by indulging in day-dreams. To squander our time in this fashion means to render our lives sterile, and talent unproductive. We become like to the fig-tree cursed by Our Saviour because it bore no fruit.

Moreover, what ought we to think of those things which we do—according to the accepted expression—"to kill time"? Are not occupations of this kind equivalent to a loss of time? To deliver ourselves up to useless babbling, to waste an afternoon in visiting without some good purpose, to read dangerous novels, though they be of great literary excellence, to fill our minds with the refuse of newspapers, all this is, I grant, an occupation; but occupations of this kind are, rightly understood, a real loss of time.

Behold now another way in which we lose time: by amusing ourselves, not for the sake of refreshment or relaxation after work, but independently of all work, merely to pass away the time pleasurably. This immoderate desire for pleasure is one of the temptations of riches, and one of the reasons, doubtless, which led Our Saviour to say that it is exceedingly difficult for a rich man to enter into the kingdom of Heaven. I often recall the text which Cardinal Langenieux chose when preaching a Lenten sermon at the Tulleries, in the reign of Napoleon III. This venerable and saintly man chose no other words than those which were repeated every morning in this frivolous court of the third empire: "How shall we amuse ourselves to-day." Self amusement was the great end of the lives of these courtiers. Take care, my daughters, that you do not bring into your lives something of these deplorable manners, and remember well that to run after pleasure is to lose the true life.

Let us consider, finally, one more way in which we lose time: by doing something other than that which we ought to do. You yield, for example, to a temptation to make some fancywork during the time set apart for an exercise of piety. You are not at all inactive during this time, nor could you be accused of idleness. But you are losing your time, nevertheless, by employing it in a manner contrary to the actual design of God.

*

*   *

What resolutions should we adopt, then, in the face of these considerations?

1. I shall never remain idle, nor lose one single instant of my time.

2. I shall draw up for myself a rule of life, adapted to my state, comprising only a few articles, and capable of being applied to the diverse circumstance of my life. I shall ask myself every evening if I have observed this rule in all its essentials.

3. I shall be faithful to the following rule which, so to speak, multiplies time, and permits even the busiest person to find time for everything. The rule is this: *I shall never put off what I can do now.*

CHAPTER V

THE NEED OF A RULE OF LIFE

ONE of the resolutions which I suggested in the preceding chapter was fidelity to a rule of life. Have you a rule of life? Do not say that a rule is possible for a religious, but impossible for the mother of a family. This is an error! Every woman, whatever her lot in life, and whatever her obligations, ought to have a rule of life. Of course, the rule of a religious will be less open to modification, and will entail greater precision and severity than yours. Nevertheless, you must have a rule, otherwise your life will be squandered in a thousand follies and futilities.

Need this rule be written? When written, it will have much more precision than if it were only in the memory. But do not imagine that it should cover many sheets of paper. A few simple resolutions, clearly stated, will be entirely sufficient. You need not overburden yourselves in the beginning. Go forward step by step. A rule is not immutable; we can always add to it according as divine grace directs us. Indeed, it is better to add to a rule than to subtract from it. It is better to begin at a moderate pace, than to be obliged to slacken our speed, and perhaps lose heart.

*

* *

Let me call your attention to the advantages of a rule of life. First, it saves you from yourselves, so to speak; from the spirit of caprice which finds its way so easily into your actions, and robs you of the greater part of your merit. We all are tempted to do only what pleases us, and to avoid sacrifices as much as possible. An act needs but to take on the appearance of duty to become an object of aversion to us. The result is that unless you are bound by a rule, your lives will drift unceasingly; they will float along guided only by caprice, and the sense of duty will be almost entirely lost. In that case it is your own will that you have followed from morning until evening, and not the will of God.

From the viewpoint of merit, what a sad life is that which is not regulated. It is a life which, from a worldly standpoint, may have a certain respectability, but which, from the supernatural side is a mere farce. Will you tell me what that day weighs, in the divine balance, during which you follow your own will with never a thought for the will of God?

The evil of our century is precisely the absence of the supernatural in life. It is this naturalism, this worldliness, that draws Christian souls back to the ideals which honest Pagans formerly conceived at Rome or at Athens. Do you imagine that you can combat this naturalism by leaving your life unbridled, so to speak, without a bit to restrain it, or a rule to regulate it? I have no hesitancy in saying that a life without a rule, is a life wherein the supernatural, that is, the part of God, has little or no importance.

Here is another advantage of a rule of life: there are many bound by a rule whose lives are very fruitful. She who lives by a rule finds time for everything. Such a life produces its effects much more quickly, and with less fatigue, than a life without a rule. Ask any Christian mother who accomplishes an astonishing amount of work, yet never has an air of depression, ask her, I say, the secret of her activity. She will tell you that she works methodically, because she is guided by her rule.

Others, though always occupied, accomplish little because they follow the inspiration of the moment. When perchance they have finished a work, they lose a quarter of an hour asking themselves what to do next. Then they attempt something, leave it unachieved because it has suddenly become distasteful to them, pass to another work, return finally to the first, and, in the end, accomplish nothing. True, they have been occupied continually, but they have been badly occupied, and have succeeded in making every one around them discontented. Now the ridiculous part of it all is this, that instead of laying the fault to themselves, they feign to be misunderstood, and accuse their husbands of not rendering justice to their tact.

*

*   *

If you desire me to draw up for you the essentials of your rule, I will say that you should first determine the hour of your rising and retiring. Do not remain undecided on this important point. The rule extrolled by spiritual writers, as well as by physicians, is to retire early in order to rise early.

Here is another article that ought to find its place in your rule: morning and evening prayers should be said kneeling. Moreover, there is hardly one among you who cannot spend a quarter of an hour each day in spiritual reading. You should have a special article binding you to that. Those of you who have the time, and who are unwilling to be satisfied with merely earthly piety, ought to take measures to make a meditation every morning, and also to attend Holy Mass each day, or at least several times during the week.

Do not forget to receive the sacraments. But

of all the articles this will be the one most subject to modification. The more often you communicate, the more ardent will your desire for the Holy Eucharist become. It will be necessary, therefore, to modify your rule more and more frequently in regard to the reception of the sacraments.

I will propose this rule for the distribution of your time. Give your attention, above all, to the most important duties. I mean those of your interior, and station in life. Then attend to the less important duties; the remainder of your time may be spent on duties of pure decorum—if any more time remains.

Since your rule has been made for God, it is for God that it should be followed out. This rule is the expression of the will of God in your regard, which must of necessity be very dear to you. Bring, then, to the accomplishment of each of these articles, a true spirit of faith, and a truly supernatural motive, and place yourselves a hundred times daily under the eye of God, saying frequently to Him with love: "All for you, My God."

CHAPTER VI

I SHALL discuss in this chapter a very practical subject, a subject demanding serious consideration. I refer to promptness in rising.

I have just informed you that this subject is very practical. I must add that it is very important. The truly spiritual life is absolutely impossible for her who is irregular in rising. If you say that you do not exert yourselves overmuch to be exact on this point, I know what to think of your exercises of piety. You probably omit them often for want of time, or perform them languidly and mechanically. But surely, my daughters, you all rise at an early hour, you are not given over to a habit of laziness. Moreover, instead of insisting on exactness and promptness in rising, I believe it is far more useful to state a few practical rules to which you should conform.

First of all rise at a fixed hour.   Decide on the time, and examine well into the effect your early rising will have on your general health and temperament.   But once this hour is fixed, make no exceptions to it, save only when sickness or extraordinary circumstances render them necessary.

How many hours of sleep are necessary? Physicians advise seven hours for a robust person; but among religious communities generally eight hours are allowed.   You may adopt this rule, but do not exceed eight hours.   You would be yielding to weakness and sensuality.   A prolonged sleep will not deliver you from an indisposition, which very often is more imaginary than real.   You complain of feeling ill at awakening, and it seems that to raise your head from the pillow is a sacrifice beyond your strength. Pay no attention to this temptation!   Give the enemy no quarter!   Rise up at once, and you will feel that your complaint was imaginary. The ancients were wont to say that life consists in movement.   You will experience the truth of these words, and you will learn how to mount to a degree of activity which you thought impossible.

＊

＊　＊

Rise early! This slogan holds the secret of a complete and perfect life. By rising early the best hours of the day will be yours; hours when the mind is clear, hours well suited for meditation. If, on the contrary, you defer your rising, an irremediable disorganization will continue throughout the day from this first fault. The intellectual and moral life of a person who rises late, Père Olivant was wont to say, is seized by an impotency like to that of the Romans at Capua. Hence the words of Holy Scripture: "My son, love not sleep, lest poverty overtake thee." Poverty? Yes, but not so much in the sense of material goods, as of the mind and heart.

How much I desire to picture to your minds, types of those stolid Christians of the early days, with their habits of virility and courage. It was not to religious, but to the simple faithful of Milan that St. Ambrose addressed these words: "You should be ashamed to have the first rays of the sun find you in bed. These early rays reproach you for the time you have lost for merit and the oblation of spiritual sacrifices. Precede the dawn, so that when the day breaks it will find you ready to take up your duties."

Would you care to know what were the habits of Christians in the sixteenth century, even of those who mingled in the highest class of society? Listen to the words of the great magistrate, Henri de Mesmes: "I was sent with my teacher to Toulouse to prepare for the profession of law. We arose at four o'clock every morning, and having prayed to God, we set out at five, our books under our arms, and our inkstands and candlesticks in our hands."

Mothers of families, are you not ashamed to lie in bed and to miss a Mass said at seven or eight o'clock, when your servant has cut short her sleep so that she might assist at an earlier Mass?

You who deem it too onerous or too common to rise at six o'clock, are you aware that in certain religious communities, it is the custom to rise at two, and often earlier, to sing matins? Let me tell you that these religious generally live to a ripe old age, and never suffer from those headaches and other indispositions of which you complain at your late rising.

Père Lacordaire, in his writings, after having branded this weakness for late rising, and pointed out its dangers, indicates the remedy for it: "To rise early, retire early."

"The man," he writes, "who prolongs his sleep beyond the early morning, because he has prolonged his retiring beyond a just limit, finds the noise and bustle of worldly affairs in his head, when he wakes. He is seized by a tumultuous uproar, and vainly does he seek from God those hours lost through his own dissipation. To-day, by a common aberration, by a too frequent reversing of the order of nature, the night is made the day, and the day, night. But nature takes revenge for this insupportable burden imposed on her, by an idiocy which saddens the imagination—an evil that was not known to antiquity. They are right, then, who say that the world belongs to those who rise early, and that those who have attained eminence during their earthly career, have succeeded only on this condition."

When we advise any one to assist at Mass or to make a quarter of an hour's meditation in the morning, the usual response is: "I have no time." Why? "Because as soon as I arise I must set about my work." But could you not rise earlier? "No, I go to bed at such a late hour." But who compels you to retire so late? "No one; it is just a habit." Ah! how deplorable is this habit. To say nothing of its ill effects on health, it tends to the ruin of piety, and paralyzes all effort towards the truly supernatural life.

What is the remedy, you ask. Retire one hour earlier at night, and the next morning you may rise one hour earlier. Physicians will

tell you that hygiene unites with religion in giving you this advice.

*

* *

In fine, rise promptly. What do you gain
by lying in bed and indulging in questionable
reveries? More than one virtue has foundered
in these moments wherein it is impossible for
the will to guide and to guard the mind.

To rise at an early hour will be irksome.
However, this sacrifice will be a very sweet act
of love to our Lord. Oh! how happy that day
is in which our first actions are stamped with
the sail of sacrifice. Be assured, my daughters,
that such a day will be replete with good works.
It will be a day in which the heart will overflow
with peace.

CHAPTER VII

VENIAL SIN—ITS UGLINESS

My daughters, one of your principal aims ought to be the struggle against venial sin. I am firmly convinced that you all have a deep detestation for mortal sin. But perhaps with many among you the hatred of venial sin is not active and direct enough. Hence I desire to place before you some of the reasons that ought to fill you with a true detestation of it.

Let me remind you first of all, that venial sin is an injury to the majesty of God. On one side of the scales we place the will of God and the respect due to His majesty. On the other side we put a spirit of vanity, sensuality and idleness. And lo! The will of God and the respect due to His majesty are found too light; the miserable pleasures which we covet are far heavier.

How rash we are when we say so glibly:

49

"Oh! it is only a venial sin." Only a venial sin! Yes, but we should say these words in fear and trembling.

"I find too many wise Christians," writes Bossuet in one of his funeral orations, "who know too well how to distinguish venial from mortal sin. What! will not the common name *sin* suffice to fill you with horror for both venial and mortal sins? I detest your vain science and your wicked subtlety. O rash Christians, who so boldly say: 'This is only a venial sin.' Those who are truly pure, truly Christians, are not so wise."

Oh, how wise were the saints who regarded venial sin from the standpoint of the injury it causes to God, and who strove to realize the gravity of the slightest fault. You will recall the answer of Maria Teresa, wife of Louis XIV, when some one made light of a fault for which she bitterly reproached herself. "After all," said this person, "it is only a venial sin." "Ah," said the queen, "every action that offends God is mortal to me."

It is in regard to the majesty of God offended

by venial sin, that Père de la Colombière has
written: "The most acute of all the angels
would try in vain to give us an adequate conception of the gravity of venial sin, since he
himself cannot comprehend it."

Our Lord one day revealed to St. Catharine
of Genoa the malice of a single venial sin. "I
know not why I am not dead," she writes,
"since I have seen the malice caused by the
slightest venial sin. Oh! if the shadow of a
venial sin has appeared so horrible to me, what
a monster must mortal sin be! I verily believe
that were it to appear to one in all its ugliness,
it would be sufficient to cause instantaneous
death. I myself have seen the malice of only
a slight fault, and this vision lasted but an instant, yet my blood grows cold even now at the
remembrance of it; I feel myself growing weak,
and I venture to say that the slightest prolonga-
tion of this horrible vision would have killed
me." . . . "All that I have just said concerning the ugliness of venial sin," adds the Saint,
"will appear difficult to believe; yet far from
exaggerating the knowledge God has given me,

I have so attenuated it that its recital seems almost a falsehood.''

*

*   *

To realize the malice of venial sin, let us place ourselves on Calvary. From this point of view venial sin appears in all its ugliness. Venial sin is not typified by the lance that pierced the Saviour's side, nor by the scourge that inflicted so many wounds upon His Sacred flesh, by the vinegar and gall which Jesus was given to drink. Our Saviour, in the hours of His agony, was tormented by a thirst which caused Him the most bitter suffering. You, like the executioners on Calvary, instead of offering Him a beverage which will quench His thirst, place to His lips the vinegar and gall of venial sin, which far from satisfying His thirst, renders it yet more intolerable.

This is what you do when you deliberately commit a venial sin. Behold your treatment of Jesus during His Passion! You are not among the numbers of His executioners, I grant; but you are one of those who cause Him to suffer.

Is it among these that you should be found?
What would you think of a son who would force
a thorn into the head of his father and say:
"This will not kill you." What would be your
opinion of a son who would spit into his father's
face and say: "That will not hurt you." Ah!
but you differ not at all from such a son, when
you commit a venial sin, and say so glibly:
"This is only a venial sin; this does not
kill."

Two conclusions should be drawn from the
doctrine that has just been set forth. The first
is that no one is ever permitted to commit a
venial sin, even if he could thereby procure for
himself or for others the greatest possible good
in the order of nature or of grace.

"Even though we could convert all sinners
and liberate all the damned from Hell by committing one venial sin, we should not be permitted to do so." (Pergmayr.)

The second conclusion is that we should never
be permitted to commit a venial sin even though
we could thereby avert the greatest imaginable
evil from ourselves or others.

It was because this truth was deeply engraved on their hearts, that the saints would not tolerate in themselves the slightest venial sin. This explains why many among them, like St. Vincent de Paul, or St. Francis de Sales, confessed daily. But we must guard against one especial error: it is not to be inferred that this doctrine is practical only for those in the cloister, or for those rare and privileged persons destined by God to a high degree of sanctity. No one, regardless of how holy she may be, can at all times avoid faults of surprise or frailty, and it is not these faults that we have in view; we speak here of venial faults committed with deliberate intent, with full advertence and consent. We are each and all bound to suppress such faults, and we need not be canonized saints to do so.

There are many pious people who, though living in the turmoil of the world, have a deep horror of venial sin. Very rarely indeed do they commit it deliberately. What these people can do, you also can do.

Let us promise our divine Lord that we will wage an energetic warfare against some fault to which we are especially addicted, and that we will strive to suppress all deliberate venial sin.

CHAPTER VIII

VENIAL SIN—ITS EFFECTS

ONE of the most regrettable effects of venial sin is the estrangement it creates between God and the soul: that cooling off, let me call it, of the friendship between God and us, which prevents our feeling entirely at ease with Him. It is so good to know that there is no cloud between God and ourselves, and to have the consciousness of intimate union with Him. What a loss is the diminution of this intimacy! It is a loss that is unknown to the lukewarm, but which the fervent dread as the greatest of evils.

God, indeed, would like to continue to show His friendship towards those who offend Him so easily, but He cannot. The want of respect and the indelicacies of these persons necessarily chill and restrain His friendship. And not only are they deprived of intimacy with God, but they also lose His choicest graces. This is but just! God measures out His graces to us according as we measure out our love to Him. True, He delights to load us with favors, but we discourage His good will by our want of delicacy. We but partly open the door which God wishes entirely opened. It is our own fault, then, if He does not enter into our hearts with all His graces.

The loss of God's choicest graces is a misfortune which we shall realize only in eternity. The first consequence of this loss, or withdrawal of divine grace, is a dangerous darkening of the intellect. Light grows dim and is often extinguished in a person who has grown familiar with venial sin.

The second consequence is a weakening of the will, which soon fails to direct the energies towards good. Venial sin is to the will, what glue would be to the wings of a bird.

*

* *

Behold another effect of venial sin is yet more to be feared: it is a step towards mortal sin. If you do not resist a slight temptation, if you have not sufficient moral courage to say *no* to the solicitations which attract you to this or that empty pleasure, do you hope to be victorious in the crisis of a grave temptation, when your whole being, carried away by a criminal pleasure, almost escapes from the guiding hand of the will?

This is the explanation of those sudden falls which people sometimes experience. Awakening, as it were, from an evil dream, they ask themselves with astonishment and consternation how they could have fallen so low. These imprudent people have grown familiar with venial sin. They have thoughtlessly steered close to the abyss of mortal sin, until, overtaken suddenly by dizziness, they have fallen to the bottom.

From the point of view of venial sin, it would be very interesting to make a study of those who have grieved Holy Mother Church by their errors and heresies. We should discover that they did not fall suddenly into that miserable state in which history reveals them to us. We would see that they began by light infidelities and that the habit of venial sin was the cause of their lamentable fall.

Was not the treason of Judas due to a series of light infidelities, and a greed for the filthy lucre against which he had not sufficiently struggled? And Luther? And Lamennais? And what shall we say of the unfortunate Loisy, whom we in our day have witnessed breaking away from the arms of Holy Mother Church? Was not the youth of these men free from reproach? Their fall remains inexplicable if we isolate it from their abuse of divine grace, their pride, obstinacy, and hypercritical trend of mind.

What distrust of ourselves, and what hatred of venial sin should not the fall of these men excite in us!

"Believe me when I say that those who are satisfied with avoiding only mortal sin, take but little pains to avoid it. To keep just on the edge of mortal sin, and permit ourselves all indulgence that is not forbidden under a heavy penalty, is a most dangerous method of procedure. If you imagine that you know some people who succeed in this course of action, be assured that you are deceived, for they would have found the means of reconciling God and the world, an impossible thing according to the words of our Saviour." (Père de la Colombière.)

You whose aim has been solely to avoid mortal sin, are you certain that you have never exceeded the limit which separates venial from mortal sin? Indeed, is this limit always so easy to determine? Is it not frequently vague and obscure? Perhaps you are indelicate in the matter of charity. Perhaps you have a tendency to criticize your neighbor, and to show your fondness for raillery towards her. You guard against only one thing,—mortal sin. But when a theologian of consummate knowledge often hesitates to decide which slander is grave and which light, what right have you to form a judgment, and how do you dare to affirm that these intemperances of language to which you have so often yielded, were not such as to injure your neighbor's reputation? Were I in your place I should be greatly concerned. I should not rely too much on the intention I had of not committing a mortal sin, but should regard the actual injury committed.

Now it is very easy for this injury to be grave, and, consequently, it is very easy to exceed the limit separating venial from mortal sin. This consideration ought to deter you from thinking lightly of venial sin, and acquaint you with the utter want of reflection in this lame excuse which you so often advance: "Oh! it is only a venial sin."

I wonder if you will say that, when the flames of Purgatory envelop you. "I once saw a man cutting wood on a mountain side," writes the venerable Père Dupont, "and I asked him why he was doing so. He replied: 'I am gathering this wood to build a fire to burn myself.' I judged, and justly so, that this man was insane; but am I not more insane than he when I commit acts which will feed the flames commissioned by God to purge me from my sins?"

Remember that according to the teaching of theologians the lightest pain in Purgatory far exceeds the most intense suffering here on earth, and this thought will henceforth suffice to check these words: "It is only a venial sin."

Under the eye of Jesus, examine your conscience to see what your attitude is towards venial sin, and especially towards a habit of venial sin. Are you not still tolerating in yourselves a habit of this sin? Do not excuse your indolence by saying: "My temperament is the cause of it. After all I do not sin mortally, and therefore I am always in the friendship of God."

Determine clearly the method you will adopt in your struggle against a certain habit of venial sin, and tell Jesus of your weakness. Tell Him the principal evil from which you suffer, and of which you desire to cure yourselves, with the help of His grace.

CHAPTER IX

My daughters, I seek an answer to a most important question: *Why do we not advance?* The subject is too broad to be treated in one chapter, so we shall divide it.

Here is the first answer: We do not advance because we are ignorant of the things we ought to know. We do not advance because our intelligence is not sufficiently enlightened, that is, we do not possess, in an adequate degree, the science of the things of God.

Are you fully aware of the importance of light in the spiritual life? If you ask me what relation there is between clear knowledge and progress in the matter of spirituality, I will tell you in one simple sentence: *Knowledge always precedes love.*

Suppose, for example, that you have before you the most beautiful picture in the world; if you close your eyes so as not to see it, or if, on account of some distraction, you see it obscurely, will you love it? Never! It would be impossible for you to love it under these conditions. Again, if after partly opening your eyes you close them again, or direct them towards some other object, will you love this picture? Perhaps, but how superficially! You have not sufficiently regarded the object before you; you are not well enough acquainted with it to admire it, to say nothing of loving it.

Let us apply this principle to our subject. However admirable and worthy of love God may be in Himself, and whatever admiration and love the things of God may merit, you will love God, and the things of God, only when you know Him and then in the measure in which you ought to know them.

Here I must anticipate a false interpretation of my words. From what has been said pray do not conclude, that spiritual progress is intended only for the learned, and that in order to strive for perfection, it is necessary to possess a mighty intellect and profound learning.

There are two kinds of knowledge. The one resides in the mind and consists in merely knowing one's religion. This sort of knowledge is worth little or nothing. If it does not stimulate the heart and direct the conduct, it will be a source of condemnation.

The second kind of knowledge is that which is acquired by meditation, that is to say, by fixing the mind on the things of God and contemplating them seriously and profoundly; but above all, it consists in loving them. Now the poorest servant who knows neither how to read or to write is as capable of acquiring this knowledge as the most learned doctor. Certain geniuses like St. Bonaventure, or St. Thomas, have possessed this knowledge in all its fulness, but a poor menial in their convent could have attained it as well as these princes of the Church. For example, it is related that a poor servant to whom St. Bonaventure had expounded the truth that I have just set forth, ran to every one whom he met, crying out in his excess of love: "Do you know that I can love God just as much as our great theologian, Brother Bonaventure?"

This humble servant loved God as much as the great Bonaventure, because he had acquired that knowledge of God which is founded on prayer and meditation.

My daughters, we are all capable of acquiring this knowledge, regardless of our degree of intellectual culture; and if your progress in the spiritual life has been slow or insignificant, it is due to the fact that you have not sufficiently known God nor the things of God.

Let us now consider the principal points of this knowledge.

Do you reflect profoundly on your dependence upon that God who has given you life, who conserves it, and in whose hands you rest like a crystal globe which would break into a thousand pieces were that hand withdrawn? How important it is for you to know your true situation relative to God, you must remember that he has every right over you, and that in relation to Him you have only duties! How necessary it is for you to be convinced that His presence envelops you on all sides, that His eye follows you everywhere, and that nothing of your inmost life, thoughts, desires or affections, can ever escape that infinitely penetrating eye!

My daughters, do you consider well what your lives would be, what a great change they would undergo, if these fundamental truths were profoundly engraved on your minds? Do you not know that they would direct your conduct, and hold you unceasingly in your place relative to God?

Are you well acquainted with Jesus Christ? Do you meditate on His mysteries? Do you study that Heart which inspired all His actions? Are you convinced that the Incarnation, the Redemption and the Holy Eucharist are proofs of His love? Do you center your thoughts especially on the Eucharist? Does It arouse an immense gratitude in you? Oh, if we had a profound knowledge of what the Eucharist really is, we should be astonished that the entire universe does not bow down in adoration before the tabernacle. But alas! is not Jesus in the Sacred Host a stranger to many among you, my daughters? Is not the manner in which you treat Him after Communion a sad fulfillment of the words of St. John: "He came unto His own, and His own received Him not"?

Permit me to acquaint you with a very important subject for meditation. I refer to the supernatural life, the life of grace that is within you. The angels contemplate with ecstasy the marvelous operations of grace in your souls. They are astonished at the goodness of that God who gives to His creatures the treasure of all treasures, divine life. And do you ever give it a thought? Seldom if ever do you reflect on the fact that grace has deified you, and yet more seldom do you center your eyes on those marvels of grace which are continually taking place in your souls.

How astonishing it is that you take so little pains to augment divine grace in your souls? How strange it is that you do not use all the prudence necessary to guard and protect this treasure.

My daughters, let us now make a serious examination of conscience, and be convinced that if we have not advanced in the spiritual life, it is owing to the fact that our knowledge of God and divine things has been very insufficient. Let us promise our Lord that we shall strive to acquire this knowledge by serious meditation on all the great truths which have just been expounded. Let us strive to know God better, so that we may love Him more ardently.

CHAPTER X

(Concluded)

In the preceding chapter we have sought an answer to the question, "Why have we not advanced?"

We found that we have not advanced because our intelligence was not sufficiently enlightened, and because we have been ignorant of those truths which we ought to know.

Here is another answer to the question. We have not advanced because the heart has been attached to a thousand futilities that serve but to turn it away from God. There is one infallible means of knowing what we love, and where the heart is. Let us ask ourselves what is the habitual object of our thoughts. We think and ponder easily on whatever we love. According to this principle can we say that we love God?

Do we think of God frequently in the course of the day?   Is the thought of God familiar to us? Is it our habitual thought, our dominant thought, the thought that mingles in all our actions, and presents itself to the mind as soon as we cease to give our attention to the duties of our state or profession?

Alas! we think of every one else during the day save God.   We pass hour after hour recalling some past conversation with a friend, asking ourselves what an impression we made on her, rejoicing over a slight success of vanity, grieving over the most trifling discomfiture to our self-love, contriving the means for procuring some distraction or pleasure, and striving to attain some distinction which will flatter our pride.

Now what place has the thought of God in such a life as this?   What place does His love hold in a heart thus invaded and burdened by so many futilities and vanities?

Is it any wonder that a person of this type, passionate for everything except God, remains cold and indifferent when we speak to her of spiritual progress and advancement in virtue? She deceives herself when she says that these trifling attachments are not culpable in themselves, that they neither interfere with the essential order nor prevent an intimate friendship with God. This may be true, but it is none the less true that these attachments chain the soul to the earth and prevent it from soaring into the realms of divine love. "Whether the bird be held by a thread or a rope," says St. John of the Cross, "it is not less a captive."

Conclusion: If we are not guided and stimulated by the love of God, if we remain entangled in the silly vanities which fetter us to the earth, we shall never make progress in the spiritual life. We may never, perhaps, be guilty of grievous sin, but of this no one can be certain; for a person who does not love God, easily yields to temptation. Of this, however, I am certain: we shall never reach a high degree of sanctity; we shall always remain of the earth earthy.

How shall we acquire this love of God? First, we must desire it ardently, and, certainly, there is not one among you, my daughters, who would not desire it, did she know the great good it brings to the soul, and how a life is transformed, deified, and, I might add, beautified by it. Yes, this love which you have cast aside for other loves,—vain phantoms and shadows—this love alone can fill your souls to overflowing, and satisfy your innate need of loving and of being loved.

Ask any one who has had the happiness of finding God in any given moment of her life, and she will tell you that before she was acquainted with divine love, she was ignorant of true happiness, and that for one moment of this love she would willingly give all the pleasure and happiness most envied and sought after by the world.

To those among you who have never drunk of the inebriating cup of divine love let me address the words of the Saviour to the Samaritan woman: "If you but knew." Yes, if you but knew what a source of happiness that love would be to you, you would unceasingly beg of God to give you to drink of the water of life.

*

* *

After having looked into the heart that loves, I look into the heart that desires to love, and I find there another reason why our progress has been so slow. We do not know how to use the will, or rather we will in too vague and fugitive a manner.

For example, after a retreat or under the strain of some trial which has awakened us from our spiritual torpor, we have resolved to approach nearer to God, and to allow more of the supernatural to flow into our lives. But this resolution was forgotten twenty-four hours after it was made. Why? Because it was too general; because, though determining the end to be attained, it was entirely unconcerned with the means to attain it. Now this is the great fault with our resolutions: they are not specific enough. I desire to be more pious . . . I desire to love God more . . . I would like to become more virtuous . . . I must fulfil better the duties

of my state, words, words, mere words. You
can make these same resolutions daily for fifty
years without advancing one step. What you
must do is to study the means to be more pious,
to love God better, to be more virtuous, to fulfil
better the duties of your state, and then resolve
to use these means, not in five days from now,
not to-morrow, but this very day, this very hour,
this very moment. What you must say is this:
I am going to perform, to the best of my ability,
this or that exercise of piety which is irksome to
me.   I am going to keep silence in such and such
a circumstance, instead of displaying my temper
by angry words, and bestowing choice sarcasm
on that person whom I do not like. I am going
to acquit myself with a will of this or that duty
which is difficult for me. This is the form that
your resolutions must take to be practical, and
on this condition only will they be efficacious.

Will with perseverance! Never abandon
your resolutions because you are unsuccessful.
You perhaps have suddenly fallen after taking
a resolution that to you appeared most firm.
Why be cast down, discouraged, and groaning

over your misfortune? Ah! how much pride is often found at the bottom of those vexations which follow upon your falls!

A person who is truly humble, instead of feeding on grief, rises at once, and, relying more on the mercy and goodness of God than on her own strength, takes up the march again. To learn to profit by our falls is one of the secrets of perfection, and an essential requisite of spiritual progress.

Perhaps at this very moment there dwells in the depths of your souls, in some secluded corner where you dislike to shed light, an attachment that holds you away from God, and paralyzes your efforts to reach up to Him. If so, take the resolution now to hew down every barrier, however great it may be, which prevents the soul from intimacy with God.

CHAPTER XI

AFFECTIONS AND AVERSIONS

UNDER a different title, I shall now write a sequel to the two preceding chapters. Our spiritual life can deteriorate under the action of certain ferments of disorder which we shall proceed to study.

The spiritual life may be disordered first by *dangerous* affections. I do not say culpable affections. I say dangerous affections: and I have purposely used this word *dangerous,* so that I may be perfectly understood.

By a dangerous affection I do not mean one that is criminal in the worldly sense, for the reason that it is not followed by any exterior fall. But we must call an affection of this kind *dangerous* unless we are content to stand on the narrow margin of worldly honesty.

Indeed, how can we excuse this weakness of the heart which is nourished by questionable recollections, by reveries which we would be ashamed to make public, and by undue tenderness bestowed on persons who have no right to it? Perhaps no exterior fall, has followed, but there has certainly been an interior fall, or rather a series of interior falls, and I may also add, falls plainly perceived by the person herself.

Now I do not treat here of those solicitations or seductive temptations which even the holiest persons can experience of a sudden. I speak not of those disorders which can suddenly rise against their will, and which they stifle as soon as they perceive them. It is a question here of those affections the danger of which is perfectly and completely known. Even when nothing on the exterior would betray what was passing within, yet God severely judges this complaisance towards evil. He judges, and justly so, that the heart, weakened by an affection imprudently encouraged, is already commencing to be corrupt.

Not all at once does this virtuous woman, so austere in the first years of her marriage, begin to trifle with evil.   There has been no sudden invasion of her heart, but what is worse, a secret infiltration.   She begins by finding those pure and legitimate affections which God has been pleased to permit her, somewhat stale and monotonous.   Then, despite the warnings of her conscience, which point out the danger, and exhort her to prudence, she gives free rein to her imagination, and suffers it to be drawn aside from the path of duty.   At first, only the mind was given over to such and such a person, but the heart was not slow to become a party to this evil.   Poor, unfortunate woman!   She pretended to decide her own case of conscience, but there was too much false interest at stake for her to be loyal and unbiased, so she quickly decided that her affection was not at all culpable.

Thus, little by little, this dangerous affection took a more imperious possession of her faculties, and her entire life.

What place is there for God, I ask, in the disordered soul of this woman?   What regard can she have for the things of God, and her eternal destiny?

Let me tell you what ruin a dangerous affection works in every one who gives it free rein. It decreases piety; it silences the voice of conscience; it leads to abandonment of prayer, and finally to absolute discouragement.

In his *Introduction to a Devout Life,* St. Francis de Sales has treated this subject with all the delicacy it exacts. To it I refer those of my readers who desire to find this subject treated more at length. I shall content myself with this short extract:

"But if you are already entangled in the meshes of filthy love, good God! how difficult will it be to extricate yourself from them! Place yourself before the divine Majesty, acknowledge in His presence the excess of your misery, frailty, and vanity. Then, with the greatest effort of which your heart is capable, detest them; abjure the vain profession you have made of them; renounce all the promises received, and, with the most generous and absolute resolution, determine in your heart never to permit them to occupy the least thought for the remainder of your life . . .

"I call upon every one who has fallen into these wretched snares: Cut them—break them—tear them; do not amuse yourself in unravelling these criminal friendships; you must tear and rend them asunder; do not untie the knots, but break or cut them, so that the cords and strings may be rendered useless; do not enter into any compromise with a love which is so contrary to the love of God." (*Introduction to a Devout Life,* Part III, Ch. XXI.)

To these counsels permit me to add one other. Abstain from all conversation which could offend the virtue of purity. I desire to insist strenuously on this delicate point. How many persons, even of pious reputation, lack reserve in their conversation, and permit themselves to indulge in jokes and pleasantries which, to say the least are questionable. If you easily enter upon these subjects it is a sign that there is something poisonous and vile in you. Your imagination is not as chaste as the imagination of a Christian woman ought to be. And since out of the abundance of the heart the mouth speaketh, it is also a sign that the heart is not pure.

If the heart is pure the tongue also will be pure.

Let me tell you the principal cause of the absence of purity in the heart: dangerous readings, such as novels, plays, and newspapers, wherein immorality is flagrant.

Do not imagine that because a woman is married she has the right to sully her mind by contact with all the impure characters which it pleases a novelist to introduce into his work, or a dramatist to place on the stage. Every woman ought to guard her mind from pollution at all times, and when her mind and heart are chaste, her language will be chaste also.

*

* *

When aversion has become a part of our character, it leads to the same end as a dangerous affection. It is, like the other, an agent of disorder. When a person with whom you are obliged to live has become insupportable to you, who can tell what great injustice you are guilty of in her regard! There are a hundred things that wound you, coming, as they do, from her.

Perhaps she herself is not at all responsible for them. A gesture, a mannerism, the sound of her voice, everything about her irritates you. If you struggle against these impressions, and compel yourselves to become master of them, I have not praise sufficient to bestow on you. I assure you that this instinctive antipathy is a source of true merit for you.

But do you really struggle against your animosity? I think not! You seem rather inclined to nurse and develop it. You apply all your false impressions to it. You revolve in your minds all those painful recollections, and you take great delight in the asperity of your rancor.

What is the result? Violent thoughts arise in your mind, and you are constantly at variance with that person whom you do not like.

In the hour of prayer when the lips are pronouncing certain formulas, the mind continues to wander to the object of your aversion. Even when saying the Lord's Prayer; "Forgive us our trespasses as we forgive those who trespass against us," you renew your resolution to be revenged against that wicked person who has made you the victim of such and such an act.

Shall I speak of the slanders, and calumnies even, to which such a state of mind can give birth? Shall I speak of those disorders which it so easily engenders? I do not believe I am exaggerating when I say that the life of a person who is dominated by an aversion of this kind, is an almost interrupted succession of faults contrary to charity—venial faults generally, but sometimes grave. Indeed, who will so flatter herself as to say that she can always arrest her will at the brink of the precipice of mortal sin?

It is possible that the object of your aversion may be one whom you are bound to respect, a superior, for example, or a person living under the same roof with you, who shares in your life, and ought to be dear to your heart. Oftentimes some trifling gossip which it would have been very easy to disregard, suddenly becomes fixed in the mind. It ends by becoming profoundly troublesome to the interior, and creating distaste for a life in common.

Why be astonished, then, that lukewarmness is the result of this disease of the soul?

*

*   *

I have said enough, it seems to me, to arouse my readers to the danger which every passion, be it aversion or affection, creates in the spiritual life. "God is not in the hurricane," says Holy Scripture. If you desire to draw nearer to God, watch over every sentiment, even those praiseworthy sentiments in you, which, by undue exaggeration, may become a cause of disorder. It will be easy for you to check the evil at the start; while you cannot triumph over it, save at the price of heroic efforts, if you imprudently permit it to develop.

The best treatment in medicine is always the preventive treatment. This same treatment is equally salutary in spiritual illness, and in applying it to the subject which occupies us, let me say that the best method of treating lukewarmness is to foresee and prevent it.

PART SECOND

THE MEANS

CHAPTER I

My daughters, let me suggest spiritual reading as a first means of becoming fervent. Under this heading I include all reading which enlightens the mind and determines the will to do good. But you must not imagine that manuals of religious instruction or works of apologetics are the best books for spiritual reading. It is light rather than edification that such books bring, and it is just the contrary that must be sought for in spiritual reading. Spiritual reading is primarily an instrument of perfection and holiness. The acquisition of knowledge, even spiritual knowledge, comes only second in importance. The field thus limited is, however, very vast: books of piety, the lives of the saints, and biographies containing useful lessons will furnish excellent material for spiritual reading.

This said, it is now my intention to show the

89

principal advantages of spiritual reading. First of all, it is a salutary pause in the hurried life which most of you lead. Your lives are very active, and filled with occupations which consume almost all your time. Do these occupations estrange you from God? Are they obstacles to perfection? No, certainly not, provided they are spiritualized by a superior principal and supernatural intention. These occupations are the duties of your state; consequently they are the expression of the will of God in your regard. Why, then, does not all your exterior activity sanctify you? Why do you complain of making so little progress, despite the scrupulous observance of the duties of your state? Why? Because there is not within you that interior life which is the soul of the exterior life; because the thought of God, the love of God, and eagerness to please God play little or no part in your lives. Thus is explained why your lives, apparently so complete, are, in reality, so barren.

You know well that I speak the truth when I touch this tender wound. How often we priests receive the confidences, I should say the griefs, of excellent mothers! These women, devoted to their duties, never shunning sacrifice, nevertheless lament because their relations with God are not what they should be. They feel that their spiritual life is at a standstill. What is needed to fill up this great and deplorable void in their lives is God, installed in their hearts, animating all their acts, and communicating to these acts a dignity and a supernatural value. To think of God only in the morning and at night, when we recite a few prayers mechanically, is indeed a poor program for the spiritual life. Can we thus attain the end for which God has created us, for which He descended upon earth, and instituted the Holy Eucharist? You understand, then, my daughters, that God must play the principal part in our lives. Hence we do great injustice to ourselves when we offer to God an exterior piety arising solely from routine.

Let me propose to you an easy means of finding, in your relations with God, this charm, this cordiality, for which you have so ardently yearned, but which have not yet found.   Devote at least a quarter of an hour every day to pious reading.   Let it take the form of a talk, an intimate conversation with God, and I promise that it will not be long before you will witness a happy change in your lives.   You will joyfully realize that these apparently vulgar actions, to which you devote yourselves each day, will take on a new form, and henceforth have a purpose. You will then taste those joys of the love of God which the saints have celebrated.   In short, spiritual reading, if methodically practised, will effect a complete transformation in your lives. You are free to use this means or to reject it; but if you reject it, you are evidently content to remain in your present barren state.   In this case cease to lament; you are not sincere.

My daughters, I now address those of you who are serious in the practice of piety, whose love of God is efficacious, and who prove this fact by binding themselves to a rule of life, approaching the Holy Table frequently, and devoting to their prayers all the time at their disposal.   To you also, spiritual reading will be of the greatest utility. It should not be merely an ornament in your lives, but rather an exercise incumbent on you despite all caprice. It constitutes one of the essential parts of your spiritual life, and I shall prove this assertion with very little difficulty.

No doubt you are aware, my daughters, that your personal wardrobe, let me say, of ideas and sentiments is not very extensive, and that unless you renew it frequently, it will soon be exhausted. Left to yourselves, you will always revolve in the same plane, think the same thoughts, and perhaps never find a new habiliment in which to dress them. Therefore, you must frequently renew your wardrobe of ideas. Some one must whisper new sentiments into your ears each day. Now spiritual reading can render you this service. The author of the pious work which you will read, plays the part of a very rich friend, who opens up his treasures and shares them with you. You will enrich yourself, then, with the spirit of the saints; you will absorb their sentiments; you will be benefited by the fruits of their experience. It is useless to insist further on the advantages of spiritual reading; you already sufficiently appreciate, I hope, the immense advantage which your natural poverty will find in this participation in the riches and wealth of the saints.

To my mind, the best and the least fatiguing of preachers is a good book. It is not importunate when you leave it, and you may return to it when you wish; it is not indiscreet, since it gives advice without knowing whether or not it will be followed; it is not susceptible to jealousy, since it accords you the liberty to reject its counsels, or to prefer those of another. It would be a grave error to believe that the preaching of a good book is intended only for those specially consecrated to God. When we exhort certain persons to do some spiritual reading every day, they look at us with astonishment and exclaim: "Do you advise spiritual reading for me, the mother of a family who has to live in a whirlwind of duties in the midst of the world? This advice would be good for a religious, or for those who live in the solitude of the cloister."

This objection is by no means new. St. John Chrysostom, in his day, answered it as follows: "What do you say? The reading of these good books does not concern you? But I find this duty more incumbent on you, than on those living in the security of the cloister. For you who sail on the open sea, whether you will it or not, are beset by a thousand occasions of sin. Thus the aid of spiritual books is for you a necessity. A religious cannot be wounded, because she is far from the combat. But you who are in the midst of battle, must protect yourself with the buckler of holy thoughts drawn from good books."

Meditate also, my daughters, on these lines which St. Francis de Sales wrote to Madame Brulart, an accomplished woman of the world: "I wish that you would not permit a day to pass without giving an hour, or a half hour, to the reading of some spiritual book." And in another letter to the same lady he says: "Read as often as you can, but only a little at a time, and, above all, read with devotion." In his *Introduction to a Devout Life,* the Saint completes this counsel: "Have always before you some good and pious book, and read a little in it each day with devotion, as if you were reading letters which the saints had sent you from Heaven, to show you the way and encourage you to follow it."

*

*   *

Why have the saints so highly extolled the advantages of spiritual reading? Why have they exalted it—almost to a level with prayer? Without doubt, they were guided by the reasons which I have placed before you; but they were influenced also by another motive, one that seems of capital importance to me. It arises from the fact that spiritual reading is one of the principal sources whence we draw light.

Have you ever reflected, my daughters, how important light is for us in our relations with God? From certain maxims or passages taken at random from spiritual writers, it would seem that mortification and sacrifice are the sole means of approaching nearer to God. Thus the author of the *Imitation* exalts reaction against our evil inclinations. He declares that the success of our struggle against nature is always the measure of our progress towards perfection.

Certainly this principle is true and it would ill become us to complaisantly modify it. On the other hand, we must remember that energy in sacrifice is dependent upon clear-sightedness. We are energetic in sacrifice only when we see clearly the object of that sacrifice. It is the office of the intelligence to point out the path to the will. The will itself would remain inert, if motives of action and sacrifice did not stimulate it. A strong and vigorous will is always accompanied by an enlightened intelligence. Must we not conclude, then, that a solid knowledge of the principles of the spiritual life is a potent aid to the soul in its striving towards good? Hence, we must appreciate the value of spiritual reading since it furnishes us with the principles of the science of the saints, as well as with practical counsels, and precious examples.

To be sure, God can, when He so wishes, dispense with every intermediary, and become

Himself the teacher of those simple and pious persons who lack intellectual culture. We have seen this in the case of that poor menial who could neither read nor write. We have learned of his great and heroic sanctity. In this case, books of piety did not bring about those marvelous results. Shall we say that this mediocre mind did not receive light from on high? No! A thousand times no! Light was directly shed upon that mind by God. And why? Because it could not be enlightened save by that means. But if you, my daughters, hope that God will employ a similar means in your regard, you will have to wait a very long time. God has given you the means to instruct yourselves in spiritual science, and you are bound to use these means. Now if the reading of pious books is one of these means, you are bound in conscience to read them.

Under pain of allowing our spiritual life to run wild, we are obliged to develop the intelligence as much as possible. Why be astonished, then, that the lives of so many persons are sterile? If they do not make progress in the spiritual life, it is due to the fact that their minds are not enlightened, and that their intellectual vision is defective. And what will rectify this defective vision? The words of a master drawn from spiritual reading. Take, for example, two persons equally endowed with intelligence: one has been in contact with the best authors through spiritual reading, while the other has always been content with her own resources. I hold that the former will travel very much faster than the latter on the road to sanctity.

I pause to answer an objection which I have frequently met with from those who do not practise spiritual reading. "Do you engage in spiritual reading every day," I have asked; and they have responded: "No! I have no time." Well, for mothers of families who toil from morning till night to gain a livelihood, this reason is acceptable; but when it is alleged as an excuse for the laziness and inertia of those who squander a considerable amount of time in useless babbling, in long and purposeless visits, and in reading the daily papers, this excuse is intolerable. How many are there among you, my daughters, who cannot reserve at least a quarter of an hour every day for spiritual reading, by omitting all futile occupations, and by economizing their time. There are some, perhaps, but not very many, I know.

CHAPTER II

In the preceding chapter, I have pleaded the cause of spiritual reading, and pointed out the immense advantages accruing from this exercise. It is now my intention to give you some practical counsels on the manner of doing it profitably.

Before opening a book, it is well to ask God in a short prayer to grant that your reading may be profitable both to the mind and to the heart. "Lord, open my mind to Thy word. Grant that I may understand it, relish it, and put it into practice." In these terms does St. Ephram exhort us to address God before we begin to read. I advise you to repeat these words, my daughters. Perhaps you have read and reread some passage in a spiritual work without ever understanding it. At least you have never penetrated into its depths, nor grasped its hidden meaning and practical con-

101

sequences. And why? Has the author written in enigmas? Have his words lacked clarity? Not at all. His thought is always perfectly expressed. If you have reaped no benefit from your reading, it is due to the fact that you have read without light from above: without that light which is absolutely necessary to give you a knowledge of the things of God. The proof of this assertion lies in the fact that, rereading this same passage to-day, you receive a sudden illumination, your minds are flooded with light, and things are revealed to you, of whose existence you did not dream. What, then, is the conclusion to be drawn, if not that, left to yourselves, you would walk in darkness, without knowledge of the truths of your holy religion. Poor blind people that we are, how needful it is for us, before opening a book of piety, to supplicate the Holy Spirit to reveal to us its true sense, by enlightening our minds on those parts which seem obscure?

*
* *

Some read solely with their minds. They

treat the science of God as a human science. Their one aim is to satisfy their need of knowledge and instruction. If you, my daughters, should attempt spiritual reading with this end in view, it would be just as well, I must avow, to lay down your book. You would only waste your time.

The author of the *Imitation* tells us that there are two kinds of knowledge. One resides solely in the mind; it is cold and sterile. The other resides in the heart, and having partaken of its warmth, is warm itself and luminous. It is this latter knowledge, impelling us to action, self-reform, and the practice of good deeds, that we must have in view when making our spiritual reading. I will read so as to learn the means for becoming better. I will seek light for my mind and yet more for my will. In one word, I will strive to know God better so that I may love Him better. Such are the intentions we should form before opening a book of piety. Let us follow the advice which St. John Baptist de la Salle gives us: "Read your book," he writes, "as you would read a letter which Jesus

Christ had sent you to make known His will, and what He expected of you.''

*

*   *

Read seriously and slowly. Take time to assimulate the thoughts of the author. These are precious counsels given us by the saints.

Now there are some people who take it upon themselves, in all seriousness, to read a certain number of chapters each day. These people conscientiously perform their task to the very last word. Whether their book of piety is easy to understand, or exacts a great amount of meditation, it is all the same to them. They have bound themselves to read just so many chapters daily. I am curious to know just how much could sink into the mind of a person who would thus swallow whole a chapter of the *Imitation*. Maxims, such as those contained in this work, must be dwelt upon in serious meditation, if we wish them to sink into the mind, and be relished by the heart. When I see a reader gulping down, let me say, the maxims of the *Imitation*, I am not at all fearful that she is expending too much cerebral effort. The poor woman has read, but she has not thought. Despite myself, I am strongly reminded of this axiom in medicine: "It is not what we eat, but what we digest, that nourishes."

My daughters, you must learn how to digest your reading. Now this digestion, this assimulation of the thoughts of others, is impossible without reflection. By this I mean that you should reread a passage several times if need be, and repeat it to yourselves until you are positive that you have grasped the thought of the authors. A spiritual book cannot be read like a novel; it requires serious meditation, since it is not a mere amusement for the mind.

These practical counsels would be incomplete, did I not exhort you to propose to yourselves a few important questions in the course of your spiritual reading. As the various truths stretch out before you ask yourselves what your convictions are, and how you stand from the viewpoint of practice. Compare your conduct with the maxims inculcated by the author, and determine the method you will adopt in reforming your lives.

CHAPTER III

I FANCY that I can hear several of my readers proposing this question: "Having resolved henceforth to do some spiritual reading, we desire to know what books you would advise us to read." The question is certainly practical, and moreover, attests, on the part of those who advance it, a certain good will which affords me great joy. But I must avow that I am at a loss just what to answer. I have assuredly come to the most arduous part of my task.

How many questions must be answered, and how many obscurities cleared away, before it may be said to any one, from a knowledge of the cause: "This is the book suitable for you." The moral temperament of a person, her particular needs, the duties incumbent upon her, the time at her disposal, the degree of spirituality which she has attained, all these facts must be taken into consideration. Therefore, on account of the difficulties which this problem involves, I shall attempt to take refuge in this response: In the matter of spiritual reading, we must consult our conscience, especially in case of doubt. In this work, destined as it is to be read by persons of all degrees of spirituality, filled with various aspirations, and pursuing paths diamentrically opposed to each other, the most I can do is to fix a few landmarks, so to speak, and give only general directions.

*

*　*

The Gospel is entitled to a special place in preference to all other books. It ought to be in every family. You should never permit a day to pass without reading at least a page of it. It is humiliating to think that Protestants must be proposed as models for you in this matter. The four Gospels are within the reach of even the poorest. They are the best reading for you and your family.

*

*　*

When a person is sure not to obtain very

much, he is usually modest in his demands. If I must deal with a person who submits with a grimace to spiritual reading, and to whom it is almost necessary to do violence to have her give a quarter of an hour a day to God, I shall be careful not to advise a book of strong spirituality. She would invariably abandon her reading after a few attempts, or her continual yawns would give an excellent idea of the fruit which her reading produces. A strong viand supplies much more nourishment to a weak stomach than is useful. My advice to such a one is to read the life of some saint, wherein the charming style, the interest of the narrative, and the profundity of the psychological analysis take the edge off the lessons of austerity. Msgr. Bougand and Msgr. Lagrange are masters in this art. A work bearing the signature of either of these two men, may always be placed in the hands of a beginner, with the certitude that the reader will be captivated as well as edified. To one who is susceptible to emotion, and who can grow enthusiastic over noble causes, I should advise the life of Père Lacordaire, by Père

Cocarne, or the biography of Henri Perreyve, by Père Gratry. Acquaintance with these heroic and sympathetic men, will make us better; detach us from the thousand vanities in which we are centred, and elevate us to those heights on which these great Christians have led their lives.

There is one book whose privilege it is to speak as a friend to any one who wishes to consult it: a book which has remedies for all the wounds of the soul, consolations for every trial, and rules of life for all imaginable situations. It is the book for the layman, as well as for the religious, for the woman of the world as well as for the recluse, for the beginner who struggles against his passions, as well as for the saint confirmed in virtue. I refer to *The Imitation of Christ*. "This book," says Fontenelle, "the best that has come from the hand of man since the Gospel, would not go straight to the heart, as it does, nor seize it with so much force, if it had not that natural and tender address, to which even negligence of style adds very much." The author of the *Imitation* is not a friend who has pruned his words. His language has not that affectedness which ordinarily characterizes human attempts at consolation. It is somewhat rude, nay rough at times, but what a tender, delicate, and disinterested soul is found under this roughness!

I distrust the praises which unbelievers bestow upon the *Imitation*. Their admiration appears entirely conventional to me. What can those chapters which treat solely of self-renouncement mean to him who has not the faith? What meaning is there for him in such chapters as "The Royal Road of the Holy Cross," or, "The Love of Jesus above all Things"? One must be a practical Christian to understand something of those theories which reverse the human order of things, and upset all worldly ideas. Let me add that in order to penetrate this book to its very depths, to understand the hidden sense of many expressions, and to grasp all those truths which the author has left understood, one must have lived the same interior life as he lived, and be familiar with the loftiest questions of spirituality.

My daughters, make the experiment. Reread the *Imitation* after a retreat or a mission. It will appear entirely new to you, and you will be forced to confess that up to this day, you have not understood it.

*

*   *

'A great number of spiritual works centre around the *Imitation*.   Limited as I am to one chapter, I must be content with a dry enumeration:

The Spiritual Combat, by Scupolis, which is said to be the *Imitation* reduced to practice.

The Introduction to a Devout Life, by St. Francis de Sales.

Christian Perfection, by Rodriguez.   This is a work of classic merit.   It is not only in a seminary or religious community that it should serve as current reading.   It is a little dry, but replete with doctrine.

The Practice of Love Towards Jesus Christ, by St. Alphonsus Liguori.   This is a delightful work, very easy to read.

The various works of Père Saint-Jure.

Meditations on the Holy Ghost, by Pergmayr.

The Way of Interior Peace, by Père de Lehen.

The Manual of Interior Souls, The School of Jesus Christ, The Interior Life of Jesus and Mary, by Père Grou.

Retreats, by Père Olivaint.

I know my readers are surprised that the foregoing list contains the name of no contemporaneous writer; but I could not cite some without slighting others—a thing which would grieve me deeply. I have confined myself to the classics, so to speak, which constitute the foundation of all spiritual writings.

If I have made no mention of works of exalted spirituality, for example, the works of St. Teresa, or St. John of the Cross, it is not because I am hostile to this kind of reading. I have excellent reasons for omitting them. In the first place, the imagination of women is too sensitive to the extraordinary phenomena recorded in these works; in other words, women are too susceptible to what is known in medicine as auto-suggestion. Moreover, these writings contain terms which are incomprehensible to her who has not the key to the mystic language.

Therefore, it would be almost a waste of time to read St. Teresa or St. John of the Cross, in the absence of this essential. The reading of a mystic work, then, should be undertaken only on the advice of an enlightened director.

CHAPTER IV

MEDITATION

I KNOW that the title of this chapter will not evoke the sympathy of all my readers. I fancy that I can hear certain ones among them crying out: "Meditation! Have you reflected well, rash author, on what you ask of us? Do not forget that you are writing for mothers of families, who are continually busy, and who, for this reason, are little acquainted with the high practices of the spiritual life. The most you should ask of us is to do some spiritual reading each day. Now you are adding meditation. This is too much! Do not waste your ink! Reserve your good counsels for the chosen few, who have more time than we."

You are mistaken, my daughters. I advise meditation for you who are tainted by indifference; for you who are as yet lukewarm. Yes,

I would induce you to make a meditation every day.

To begin with, I hold that meditation is not at all difficult for you. Again you cry out: "How can you say that? I have tried it many times, and have never succeeded." This argument has no effect on me. Your experiment has been badly made with a bad instrument, a book which was not suitable for you, I fancy. You must try again.

*

* *

Many among you, my daughters, have decided that you cannot make meditation. We shall see if you do not soon change your minds. I know that you feel no attraction for this exercise; it would surprise me if you did. Your attempts to meditate have been so weak that they can furnish no conclusion whatsoever.

If one of your children, before placing his fingers on the key-board, would tell you that he is utterly unable to play the piano, his affirmation would not convince you; you would demand a serious attempt from him. I have the right to demand the same from you, when you say that meditation is beyond your power. I have the right to exact from you a loyal and serious attempt; and if you give me this satisfaction, the cause is won. Your prejudice against this exercise will soon disappear.

If meditation required great intellectual effort, or a passionate expression of your love for God, I could understand your dislike for it. But in the face of a true and genuine concept of it, all those pretexts which are trumped up by lukewarmness and pusillanimity, disappear.

What is meditation if not a centring of the mind on one especial subject, for the purpose of perceiving it in all its diverse forms, and a dwelling upon the motives which can arouse in us the sentiments of love, hatred, desire, or regret? We meditate daily on the means to realize some worldly end, or on the success of an enterprise which we have undertaken. We then set in motion all the forces of the soul. We bury ourselves in profound reflection, to such an extent that we are oblivious to all exterior noise. Were we to reflect on the things of God, and the affairs of our soul as we reflect on the things of the natural order, should we be incapable of meditation?

An eminent cardinal affirms that no one has the right to say that he or she is incapable of meditation. "There is no man," he writes, "however ignorant, who cannot fix his thought on a grave affair, weigh the advantages or disadvantages resulting from it, and reflect on the means of securing the advantages, or avoiding the disadvantages. Will it be very difficult, then, for him to think of his last end, and to consider how much Hell is to be feared, and Heaven desired? He can well recall the service of some benefactor who took upon his own shoulders the weight of his debts. Will it be very hard for him, then, to conjure up in his mind the image of the crucified Saviour? He does not find it beyond his power to express his gratitude for a benefit received. Will it be hard for him, then, to express his love for God? But reflecting in this way, and expressing these vari-

ous sentiments, is nothing else than meditation."
(Brancarti, *De 'lO raison.*)

*
*   *

Take care, my daughters, not to fall into an error that is common in our day. The efficacy of prayer is too often estimated by the sum of emotions or sensations which it produces. When the movement of the blood grows rapid, and the play of the imagination becomes more facile and agreeable, it is supposed by many that the end of prayer is obtained, and it is not possible to pray better. But if, unfortunately, the organs of sense refuse to partake of the feast, then all is lost; prayer has lost its wings, and soars upward no more. Through obedience or complaisance, the attempt to pray is repeated for a few days; then with this decision, "I cannot pray," the whole affair is definitely settled.

This presumption is not new, since Rodriguez has already dealt with it; but it is found singularly reinforced in our epoch, by the exigencies of an almost sickly sensibility, with which directors of souls have to contend. Thus, in the face of all the ideas current around them, they must strongly insist, in their dealings with souls, on the end and purpose of prayer, and recall that its aim is not at all to administer to our organs of sense, but to determine the will to action. The wise counsels of Rodriguez on this subject are very precious. "It must frequently be recalled," he writes, "that the merit and fruit of prayer do not consist in arousing sentiments which produce a certain sweetness and sensible consolation. It is not necessary for you to experience these emotions: it suffices for you to desire them with a firm and determined will. When it pleases God to send you these sentiments, receive them with gratitude, but do not be grieved by their absence. God does not ask them from you, He requires only what is in your power. To love God in prayer with a firm will, is the true and solid love that He demands of you. This other love is a tender love that does not depend on you."

*

* *

Make a good choice of your books for meditation. A book adapted to your needs will always facilitate meditation. Now in this book, pass over the chapters which do not appear practical for you, or the reading of which is repugnant or onerous. This exercise should not deteriorate into drudgery. The idea is, that meditation, while very serious in itself, should also be attractive. Leave aside, then, those authors whose spirituality seems dry to you, and whose piety is narrow and harsh; adopt rather those authors who inspire confidence, and lead you to God and love.

Do you desire another counsel? Adopt from preference a book that takes for its theme the life of Jesus. Some authors propose to their readers subjects which are intended more for examination of conscience than for arousing piety. This is wrong! Humility, for example, will appear much more attractive if we contemplate it in the abjections of the Incarnate Word, than if it be shown to us in catalogue form with divisions and subdivisions. You will tell me that a page of the Gospel is a sufficient theme for your daily meditation. I am overjoyed to hear you say this; and let me advise you to seek no other book than this one. Moreover, do not imagine that you must confine yourself strictly to what you have read. Go out from your subject, and speak with God concerning your actual needs. Expose to Him your fears, your trials, and your hopes. In one word, make use of a holy liberty in this conversation with God. "Your prayer," writes Fenelon, "is efficacious only when you are at ease with God, your best friend in this world."

Now let each and every one among you, my daughters, decide for herself whether meditation, such as I have just described it, is an exercise filled with difficulties, and for the use of the perfect only, or whether the ease with which it can be made does not place it in the hands of all, even the lukewarm.

NOTE AND METHOD OF PRAYER.

Some one has said that the best method of prayer is that which each one has found best for himself. Thus, let me advise those of my readers who make use of any other method of prayer, to hold to the one whose advantages they have experienced. The rules that I here lay down are intended for those who have not as yet adopted a method, or who are not satisfied with the method they have followed up to this time.

Read on the evening before, the subject which you have chosen for the next day. Foresee in a general way, the thoughts on which you will pause from preference, and the sentiments which you will most easily arouse. Retire with the subject of your meditation in your mind, and recall it in the morning while dressing.

Prayer calls for three preparatory acts:

1. Adore God present around you, and in you, or better yet, go straight to the Heart of Jesus present in the tabernacle, and adore Him in silence.

2. Ask pardon for your faults. What purity does not intimacy with Jesus demand! Ask pardon for your hidden faults: "Blot out my iniquities." (Ps. *Miserere*.) Ask pardon again for the faults already pardoned: "Wash me yet more from my iniquities." (*Ibid.*)

3. Ask from the Holy Spirit the gift of prayer. "Lord, teach me to pray. . . . Grant me the gift of prayer. . . . Give me a relish for prayer, so that it may be easy for me to pray."

THE BODY OF THE PRAYER.

The body of the prayer is composed of four parts.

1. Reflection; 2. Acts or Affections; 3. Petitions; 4. Resolutions.

1. Reflection. Recall to mind the subject you have chosen. If you have already meditated often on the subject, if you are well convinced of the truths in question, or if you know all the principal points of the mystery on which you meditate, a simple recollection will suffice, and you will pass immediately to the acts. If, on the contrary, your convictions are not deeply rooted, or if you have never penetrated into the depths of this mystery, you may draw up in your minds the reasons that lead to conviction, or circumstances that will throw light on the mystery.

It is the intelligence that acts in this case.

But permit it to act only in so far as is necessary. Prayer is not a speculation nor an intellectual game; it is an affectionate conversation with God for the purpose of becoming better. Do not permit the intelligence to act, then, save when it is necessary to arouse the acts or affections.

2. The Acts or Affections. You will have a choice of various acts; but remember, that in so short a time it will be impossible to produce them all. If only one suffices, confine yourselves to it, *viz:* faith, confidence, desire, contrition, firm purpose of amendment, and the most important of all, the act of love. You must tell God that you love Him above all things. This act must result from, and terminate every meditation without exception. To supply the insufficiencies of your love, appeal to the ardent love of the Heart of Jesus.

AN IMPORTANT OBSERVATION: Do not be afraid to repeat the same sentiments to our Divine Lord over and over again. You will never tire any one by repeating frequently that you love him, and that you desire to avoid whatever displeases him.

Petition: This point merits a separate place in our prayer. Never make a prayer without a petition; be always a mendicant before God. Moreover, ask with the Heart of Jesus, and by the Heart of Jesus. And ask what?

(a) Grace to correspond to the subject meditated upon.

(b) Other graces for all that concerns you from a natural and a supernatural standpoint.

(c) An ever increasing love for the Sacred Heart.

(d) Heaven.

(e) The conversion of sinners, and the reign of the Sacred Heart over all the earth.

4. Resolutions: These should be very precise, and of such a kind that they may be put into practice that very day. It is a good idea always to renew some particular resolution. It is also well to take some particular resolution that is suggested by the subject, or adapted to

certain circumstances which you foresee will occur during the day.

Finally, place all your resolutions, and the fruit of your prayer, under the guidance of the Sacred Heart of Jesus.

CHAPTER V.

In the preceding chapter we have said that good resolutions ought to follow our prayers.

My daughters, do you know what a resolution is? Do you not often confound it with a simple desire? For example, you may have a wish to visit some friend who lives many miles away, but the difficulties of the journey prevent your undertaking it, and you postpone the project to some later date. Relative to the journey, you entertain only a simple desire. When will you have formed a resolution then? When you have determined to make the journey; when you have said: "I am going to visit that friend, and I shall set out on such and such a day."

A resolution, then, is an act of the will demanding execution at an opportune moment, while a desire is only a dream, which is cherished with more or less complaisance, but never leads to action.

127

A short analysis will suffice to show you that the resolution is one of the principal elements of spiritual progress. You make progress only in so far as you sincerely and firmly wish for progress. Even when you will have formed a grand ideal of the truly Christian life, even when, through meditation, you will have great zeal for good and for virtue, yes, even then I shall be rather uncertain as to whether your efforts have not been useless, and your time wasted. You have so many desires which remain inefficacious, so many aspirations which remain sterile! Therefore, I shall not be certain that you are in earnest until I hear you say: "I will make progress despite all obstacles and every barrier."

Have you not here before your eyes the cause of your failure in the spiritual life? You have taken the mere desire of virtue for virtue itself, and because you have felt lifted up by emotion in prayer, you have believed that the end was attained; you have believed that your ideal of the truly Christian life was fully realized. However, at the first temptation you fell miserably, and preceived that your love of God, which you thought was eternal, was only a sudden blaze.

Remember well, my daughters, that the saints are saints only because they were men and women of strong and vigorous will. So few of us to-day know how to use the will. Does this not explain why the standard of sanctity has fallen so low? The generality of men are affected by a malady of the will. Because this faculty does not guide the helm, they go on at random, and become the sport of the winds of caprice. By reason of this vacillating state, they are as incapable of great good, as they are of great evil.

I must denounce this malady of the will so as to fortify you against it, and incite you to combat it both in yourselves and your children. Teach your children from their earlier years how to will manfully, and how to make resolutions which are not mere velleities. Make them put their resolutions into practice as soon as they have made them.

Remember, my daughters, that God of Himself cannot construct our edifice of perfection. He has absolute need of the co-operation of our will. Yes, we must place as a corner-stone to that edifice, an energetic "I will." Without that, all the solicitations of divine grace are vain; they are choked by the inertia of the will. We are bound, then, to co-operate with God; and in what does our co-operation consist, if not in the resolution to co-operate with His grace?

*

* *

My daughters, let me propose a question which I know will take you unawares. However, you must make a truthful answer. Have you made a good resolution to-day? Did you say this morning: "In the course of this day I am going to mortify myself in such and such a manner? I intend to offer to God this or that thing which demands sacrifice of me. I shall strive to fulfil this or that duty to the best of my ability." Oh! happy day in which you have made resolutions such as these. And how barren the day in which you have not done so.

Perhaps some of you are among the number

of the discouraged, who, because of their infidelity to resolutions taken a hundred times, fear to be disloyal again, and so do not dare to promise God anything? Struggle against this discouragement! Form once again those same resolutions which you have broken so many times. Form them with a humble distrust in yourselves, but with a boundless confidence in God.

You who make a meditation every morning and have the happiness to communicate frequently, remember that each one of these great acts of your spiritual life entails very specific resolutions. Because they have lacked this necessary crown, your prayers and meditations have often been fruitless.

*

* *

Let me say a few words now on the qualities of a good resolution.

To begin with a resolution should be precise. How can you resolve, unless you have a clear conception of the end for which you resolve? You will only waste your time, if you make "resolutions" such as these: I wish to do better . . . I desire to correct my faults . . . I would like to acquire the virtues which are dear to the heart of Jesus, etc. These "resolutions" remind me of the story of the woman who wanted to visit Paris. This woman used to say frequently: "I would like to visit Paris very much." However, as the story goes, she took no means to carry out her desire. Though she entertained this desire for twenty years, it never brought her to Paris. Now, if a person really wishes to go to Paris she will evidently decide on the day of departure, the mode of travel, and the course to take. This is the same as saying: "He who wills the end, wills the means." If you really desired to correct your faults, you would not make such vague resolutions. You would seek out the means that tend towards the end in view, and when you had discovered the road, you would say: "I must take that road."

Your resolutions must be practical. You know from experience that long-dated resolutions amount to nothing. I might even add that they betray a disloyalty on the part of those who make them. "I desire to reform, but I shall begin in a week from now." It would be so much better to say: "I do not wish to reform at all." This would be harsh indeed, but true. Sincere resolutions ought to be put into practice not in a week from now, not to-morrow, but this very day. If not, they are useless.

Your resolutions ought to be constant. To vacillate, to jump from one resolution to another, to undertake the reform of one fault to-day, and give your attention to some other to-morrow, means certain failure. You will attain serious and lasting results in the spiritual life, only by directing your forces towards one end. Dispersion of the energies engenders a fatal sterility. Recall to mind the words of the *Imitation:* "If you succeed in overcoming one fault each year, you would soon be a perfect man." Do not hesitate, then, to dwell for a long time on the same field of action, and to take the same resolutions daily, varying them according to circumstances.

Force yourselves never to begin a day with-

out making one or more good resolutions.
Then, give your resolutions a precise form.
Finally, determine that particular fault on
which your efforts must be centered, until they
have attained a decisive result.

CHAPTER VI

My daughters, weigh well these words of an esteemed ascetic writer: "We cannot pretend to honesty in the perfect life, if we do not practise examination of conscience with exactness. We can indeed be very imperfect and not be aware of it, unless we are guided by a rule. On the contrary as soon as we adopt a rule, we can easily perceive our defects. Now, in the examination of conscience, we employ a rule by which we scrutinize our actions so as to discover whether they approach near or fall short of the straight path of duty. An artisan must always have his rule in his hand if he aims at producing a masterpiece. This is even more incumbent on the spiritual artisan, if he aims at producing a masterpiece in the supernatural order.

"When we clean a room, we gather up all the dust and dirt and then sweep it out. We should clean our spiritual room in the same way. Examination of conscience gathers up all the faults; repentance sweeps them out. We must know our faults so as to gather them up in a heap, as it were, in the memory. Finally, this knowledge should enable us to confess them, combat them, and cleanse the soul from them." (Alvarez de Paz.)

*

* *

With the writer whom I have just quoted, let me advise my readers to practice examination of conscience. This exercise seems difficult to some Christians. When we urge them to adopt it, they exclaim: "What are you proposing, a Chinese puzzle? Do you ask us to remember all we have done in the course of a day? Do you ask us to review all the thoughts which have passed through our minds from the rising of the sun to its setting, all the sentiments of affection or hatred, and all the movements of sadness or joy, which have arisen in our souls? How can you ever expect us to do all this?"

To these words we must respond: "Please

do not exaggerate.   You know full well that you are not asked to review the entire day in every detail.   There are a thousand thoughts, a thousand sentiments, a thousand products of your interior activities, which have left no trace on the memory, and which it would only fatigue you to recall.   Examination of conscience consists not so much in the perception of details, as in a general review.   There is no need of examining successively each one of the actions with which the day is filled.

Do you wish me to draw up for you a few questions, which, save for slight variations, will serve you in making a good examination of conscience?

1° Have I observed the rule for a pious life which I have drawn up for myself?

2° Have I kept up the struggle against that particular fault which I purposed to correct?

3° Have I acquitted myself conscientiously of that duty of state which I have a tendency to neglect?

Now, my daughters, is there one among you who cannot give five minutes every day to the consideration of these questions? Who, then, will longer strive to screen her laziness behind a faulty memory, or a want of time.

Many persons are astonished when they are told that an examination of conscience can last ten minutes or more. What can we do in this time, they ask? We can discover what sins we have committed during the day in two or three minutes.

These people are mistaken in the purpose of the examination of conscience. They imagine that it ought consist merely in searching out faults. This is an error. The examination of conscience ought to be a halting place in our lives during which time the soul should hold the most intimate intercourse with God.

Here is a method for an examination of conscience, drawn up by St. Ignatius.

1° Begin by thanking God. Why thank Him? Because remembrance of the benefits which God has heaped upon us, gives us a better idea of our ingratitude towards Him.

Fix your attention each day on one of the general benefits of God: creation, conservation, the Incarnation, the Redemption, the Eucharist, and the happiness of Heaven.

Finally, call to mind some one particular benefit of the present day.

2° Ask God for the grace to know yourselves well, and to judge yourselves in the same light in which He judges you.

3° Examine yourselves on the particular fault which you have determined to correct. If you wish, you may think upon the means for acquiring some virtue.

4° Ask pardon of God for your dominant fault, and ask Him to strengthen in you the hatred of venial sin, and the resolution to avoid all imperfection. In other words, ask your Divine Lord to grant you grace to co-operate generously with His inspirations.

5° Impose a penance on yourselves for the negligences which this examination has revealed to you.

Five or seven minutes will suffice for all this.

*

*   *

My daughters, do you desire to make your examination of conscience easier and more fruitful? Force yourself, then, in the last moments of your examination, to foresee the diverse circumstances which will arise during the day; seek out what temptations or difficulties you must face; then arm yourself by prevision against the attacks which you are likely to encounter, and take refuge in the resolution to wage a good fight for God.

We do not take care to foresee the attacks nor to fortify our weak points: this is why the enemy slips into our fortification so easily. We fall most often by surprise: we know that from experience. The examination of conscience, when conducted with foresight, will fortify us against surprises and baffle the ruses of the demon. As soon as any one puts this counsel into·practise with perseverance, it is easily perceived how quickly her venial sins and involuntary imperfections diminish. Her habitual somnolence and dangerous improvidence cease to become the accomplices of temptation; and her supernatural life, disentangled from the thousand meshes which fetter it, soars rapidly upward.

CHAPTER VII

THE ART OF RISING AFTER WE FALL

VERY many of us do not know how to rise up again when we have fallen. Yet, this art of rising after a fall has a very important place in the spiritual life. It is a guarantee of perseverance for those who are masters of it.

What is perseverance, my daughters? Does it mean that we never fall? No, indeed! It is the rising again as soon as we have fallen. It is the attempt to march onward towards the goal, without losing any time in lamenting our falls.

*

* *

Here is the history of many among you, my daughters. After a retreat, or an unusually good confession, you have set out with a quick step, full of confidence, and whispered to yourselves: "At such a pace I shall cover a great distance." But at the very first obstacle, at

141

the moment when you least expected it, you
have fallen flat to the earth.   Instead of rising
at once, as your good sense prompted you to do,
you have remained fixed to the earth, plunged
into discouragement, and have not dared to turn
your face towards God.   Here you are, for the
moment, numbered among the helpless people
who imagine that they can never take up the
march again.

Let us try to find out the secret reasons for
this condition.   At first sight, this self-distrust
takes on the guise of humility; but in reality, it
is only the counterfeit of this virtue.

Justly does St. Francis de Sales ridicule those
who desire to be as impeccable as the angels,
and who are not far from believing that they can
attain that end.   When these people, awakening
from their dream, find themselves with their
faces to the earth, they are utterly at a loss to
comprehend their situation.   They become
vexed with themselves, and immediately give up
the struggle.   "These emotions," says Père
Grou, "are the effects of self-love, more per-
nicious than the fall itself.   We are astonished

when we have fallen. This is a grave error!
It is a sign that we do not know ourselves. We
ought to be surprised not to have fallen more
often and into graver faults. Oh, how troubled
we are when we fall into some fault! We lose
all our interior peace, and become entirely discouraged. This discouragement lasts for hours,
for days even, and, in some cases, become fixed.
It is one of the effects of self-love, that is all.''
(*Maunel des Ames Interieures,* Ch. XX.)

What an injury is done to God by this discouragement! What a want of knowledge of
the Heart of Christ is shown by the mournful
and despairing attitude of those who, after committing perhaps a light fault, dare not look
either towards Heaven or the tabernacle.
Nothing offends Jesus more than this ignorance
of His tenderness towards sinners.

*

* *

Let us now consider the rules laid down by
the saints in regard to this deplorable state.

They bid us commence with the resolution to
struggle valiantly, and to keep in mind our

weakness. They would have us foresee all the faults that we shall probably commit in the course of our progress. Our programme of action must be clearly laid out for the moment when a fall may occur.

Perhaps it has occurred; we have fallen. What do we purpose to do? Let us remember the words of St. Paul: "With those who love God, all things tend towards good, even sin." Are you aware that evil often tends to augment divine grace in the soul? This is true, however! Your own personal experience attests it.

St. Francis de Sales indicates a practical means for profiting by each one of our falls: "Believe me, Philothea," writes this admirable Saint, "as the mild and affectionate reproofs of a father have far greater power to reclaim his child than rage and passion; so when we have committed any fault, if we reprehend our heart with mild and calm remonstrances, having more compassion for it than passion against it, sweetly encouraging it to amendment, the repentance it shall conceive by this means will sink much deeper and penetrate it more effectually than a fretful, injurious, and strong repentance.

If, for example, I had formed a strong resolution not to yield to the sin of vanity, and yet had fallen into it, I should not reprove my heart after this manner: "Art thou not wretched and abominable, that, after so many resolutions, hast suffered thyself to be thus carried away by vanity? Die with shame. Lift up no more thy eyes to heaven, blind, impudent traitor that thou art, a rebel to thy God." But I should say compassionately: "Alas, my poor heart, behold we are fallen into the pit we had so firmly resolved to avoid! Well, let us rise again; let us call upon the mercy of God, and hope that He will assist us to be more constant for the time to come, and let us enter again the path of humility. Let us take courage and from this day onward be more carefully upon our guard; God will help us; we shall do better"; and on this reprehension I would build a firm and constant resolution never more to relapse into this fault, using the proper means to avoid it by the advice of my director." [1]

* *Introduction To a Devout Life*, Part 3, ch. IX.

Remember how infinite is the tenderness of Jesus towards sinners. Instead of regarding Him as a severe judge, regard Him rather as a father, whose arms are stretched out to draw you to his heart. If your fault is grave, hasten to seek absolution from the priest. If it is but light, remember that a confident look towards Jesus will amend for it. Say to Him: "Pardon me, O my God!" Then take up the march again without losing a moment in bewailing your fall.

Listen to these words of Père de la Colombière, who was an eminent master in the spiritual life, and who, as you know, was the director of the Blessed Margaret Mary. His words seem like an echo from the Sacred Heart of Jesus. "If I were in your place," he wrote to a friend who was very much troubled over a fall, "I should console myself in this wise. I should say confidently to God: 'Lord, behold a person who is in this world to exercise Thine admirable mercy. Other people glorify Thee by showing forth the powers of Thy grace, and by this fidelity and constancy I will glorify Thee by making known how great is Thy mercy towards sinners and how Thy mercy exalts itself above all malice. I shall prove that Thy mercy can never be exhausted, and that no relapse, however disgraceful and criminal it may be, can lead me to despair of it. I have offended Thee deeply, O my loving Redeemer; but my offense would be still greater, were I to commit the horrible outrage of imagining that Thou art not merciful enough to forgive me. The demon may cause me to lose everything else, but he can never rob me of hope in Thy mercy. Though I fall a hundred times, and though my crimes be a thousand times more horrible than they are, yet will I hope in Thy mercy.'—After addressing our Lord thus, I would commence to serve Him with more fervor than ever before, and with the same tranquillity as if I had never offended Him.'' (Letter 89.)

*

* *

Let us now take the case of one who makes use of the method just indicated, but who never attains any appreciable results. Some slight fault from which she has striven to free herself, and which she imagines she has reduced in some measure, suddenly springs up again. She begins to believe that she is no farther advanced than when she began. Will she, for this reason, doubt the mercy of God, the efficacy of prayer, and the reality of the efforts she has made? If so, she will err vehemently. God has excellent reasons for leaving her in her spiritual infirmities. When God thus confronts her with failure, when He permits her to break resolutions which she has made a hundred times, He shows more mercy than if He accorded her impeccability. This poor woman must be cured of her foolish pride, otherwise she will never attain to intimate union with God. Now then, when God permits her to fall into these miserable temptations, He disillusions her mind and makes her realize her interior misery. He cures her of this swelling of pride by a treatment which, though very painful, has a sovereign efficacy.

A holy Sister of the Order of the Visitation writes: "Though you might deplore the ravages which a great flood had caused, would you not rejoice, if it had left on your land some excellent stones which you could use for the foundation of a superb palace? Now, humility is the foundation of the spiritual edifice, and God, who is its builder, can never erect it, until we have hollowed out for Him a great excavation by a true knowledge of ourselves.'' (Sister Cortelot, *Année Sainte de la Visitation*, 14 Nov.)

Let us listen to this dialogue of a saint with a person whom he was directing:

''I tell you that you will be faithful, if you are humble.

''But shall I be humble?''

''Yes, if you will to be humble.''

''But I will it.''

''Then you are humble.''

''But I know I am not.''

''Then I am sure that you are, for that is a sure sign of humility.'' (*Lettre à une Superiéure Carmélite.*)

My daughters, two resolutions should result from our little study. First, resolve to practise after each one of your falls, this prompt and confident rising again, which I have described to you. Secondly, resolve that instead of being vexed with yourselves when your efforts to triumph over a fault have been unsuccessful, and instead of losing hope, you will renew the struggle, more distrustful of yourselves, and more confident in the Heart of Jesus.

CHAPTER VIII

THE INTERIOR LIFE

"The interior life"—these are the words which the fervent among you understand, but which means nothing, or have a dreaded sense, to the lukewarm.

Now, if I were to tell you that the interior life consists simply in placing yourselves under the eye of God each day, and living in His Presence, you would no longer misunderstand the title of this chapter, nor have visions of those moral tortures which are in use in the most austere monasteries. Well, the interior life is nothing more than the exercise of the presence of God. St. Francis de Sales calls this exercise, "the most efficacious means for procuring the spiritual advancement of the soul." Consequently, it is the most efficacious means for combating lukewarmness in all its forms.

You should read in the *Introduction to a*

Devout Life, the two chapters* which St. Francis de Sales has consecrated to this subject. In his graceful and attractive style, he describes this exercise of the presence of God, and, though his analysis is very complete, he does not exaggerate the difficulties of the exercise. He contents himself with celebrating its advantages, and promises agreeable surprises to those who decide to practise it.

But St. Francis de Sales was addressing a fervent woman, who loved to retire within herself, seek God in and around her. She was one who could keep silence, and yet speak a thousand affectionate words. Now it may happen that I am dealing with a lukewarm woman. I must then fit this method of St. Francis' to her spiritual state. I shall say to this lukewarm woman: You find it difficult, you tell me, to place yourself in the presence of God every day. You complain of having no attraction for this practise. You perform it without any joy or enthusiasm. You are tempted to lay down your arms, and imagine that this in-

* Part II, chapters XII and XIII.

terior life was never intended for you. Do not yield to this temptation, I pray you. Approach near to God by your will: by duty, not by inclination.

In certain attacks of sickness we have no appetite. The very sight of food gives us nausea. Nevertheless, the doctor commands us to eat. We yield to his command through a sense of duty. First we eat to be obedient, then, little by little, the appetite returns, and we eat because we are hungry.

This same thing often happens in the spiritual life. You must place yourself under the eye of God every day out of obedience to your spiritual doctor. You must make aspirations even though they seem cold to you. Put all your good will into them, and you will soon awake from your torpor. You will begin to feel an attraction for this kind of prayer. I even dare to predict that the exercise of the presence of God will become—sooner than you think—an inperious need, and a very sweet habit.

Moreover, suppose that you should have to perform this exercise without relish all during life; suppose that you should be obliged to constrain the will in order to lead it to God, what difference would it make? Many holy persons are obliged to exercise this same violence over themselves. To many, prayer brings neither joy nor consolation. God subjects them to this trial; but it never prevents them from being very dear to the Heart of Jesus.

Let us not forget that true fervor and true love of God reside especially in the will. Let us not forget that a prayer in which we have felt no sensible attraction may nevertheless be an excellent prayer, if we have made a valiant struggle against distractions, and placed ourselves under the eye of God. In one word, let us not forget that, unlike human love, the love of God has no need of being felt; let us remember that it resides especially in a firm purpose of adhering to God, of giving Him a large share in our lives, and of accomplishing, in everything, His thrice Holy will. The conclusion is that in our attempts to approach nearer to God, and to keep oursevles within His presence, we must not be discouraged if we feel no agreeable emotions, nor think that we have lost our time if we express our love, or rather our desire to love, in terms which appear cold, and even rude. These attempts at intimate conversation with God are not at all unsuccessful: they are extremely profitable.

*

* *

There are several ways, equally good, of placing ourselves in the presence of God. First, with the eye of faith, we can see God in everything. Yes, this great God everywhere envelopes us with His presence, He is in the air we breathe. He is in the grain of sand which we tread under foot. Hence the words of St. Paul: "In Him we live, and move, and have our being."

Do you desire to seek God in yourselves? You will find him present in your hearts. This is by no means an idle fancy, for the heart, if it is adorned with santicfying grace, is the temple of the Triune God, and a sanctuary in which you can always enter into communion with the three adorable Persons of the Holy Trinity. Do not imagine God present in the heart as on a throne, receiving the homage of his vassals. Though this idea may be exact, it paints but one aspect of the reality. Imagine God present in you as a friend receiving hospitality, and profuse with his gifts.

Do you often think of God hidden in our tabernacles? This is an excellent thought for interior contemplation. What matters the distance which separates you from Jesus? Does not His infinitely penetrating eye pierce the walls that intervene between you and Him? In reality, you are continuously living under the eye of Jesus. When you converse with Jesus as if you were before the tabernacle, you are practising interior contemplation under a strictly theological and very consoling form.

Let me close this chapter by a counsel borrowed from an excellent spiritual author: "Do not despise exterior means: to kneel, to regard a pious image, to kiss the crucifix frequently and tenderly, to pray with the hands folded, to turn towards a church where Jesus is present in the Sacred Host, all these actions have their influence on the senses and arouse holy emotions. Do not impose on yourselves any penance that is too difficult for you will soon abandon it; but take care not to reject, under this pretext, every penance that is irksome. Remember that a sick person sometimes has to make an effort even to breathe.''

CHAPTER IX

No one has described better than the Apostle St. James, how great a power the tongue has for good or evil in our spiritual life:

"If any man offend not in word, the same is a perfect man. He is able also with a bridle to turn about the whole body.

"For if we put bits into the mouths of horses, that they may obey us, and we turn about their whole body.

"Behold also ships, whereas they are great, and are driven by strong winds, yet are they turned about by a small helm, whithersoever the force of the governor willeth.

"Even so the tongue is, indeed, a little member, and boasteth great things. Behold how small a fire kindleth a great wood.

"And the tongue is a fire, a world of iniquity. The tongue is placed among our members, which

158

defileth the whole body, and setteth on fire the wheel of our nativity, being set on fire by hell.

"For every kind of beasts, and of birds, and of serpents, and of the rest, is tamed, and hath been tamed by man.

"But the tongue no man can tame; a restless evil, full of deadly poison.

"By it we bless God and the Father: and by it we curse men, who are made after the likeness of God.

"Out of the same mouth proceedeth blessing and cursing. My brethen, these things ought not so to be." (St. James, Ch. III, verse 2-10.)

Which of the two, man or woman, guards the tongue better, and suffers less from a prurience to speak? This is an odious question which I shall not venture to answer. I shall leave it to those moralists who are more solicitous to give point to an epigram than to observe facts. It is relatively easy to ridicule woman's excessive desire to talk, and her horror of silence. But a man who might have at his service the wit of Rabelais, or the cunning humor of La Fontaine, would not be a fair judge in a debate of this kind. Therefore the simplest way out of the difficulty is to confess that this prurience to talk is a defect of human nature, and a temptation which all of us, men and women alike, must vigorously combat.

What is the aim of that woman who gives herself up to continual babbling? Her aim, of course, is to shine among her acquaintances, to win their esteem, and compel their admiration. But she often finds that she has attained a result diametrically opposed to that which she sought. If she is wise, she can often read on the faces of her listeners, those words which were uttered in the time of Cicero: "Empty barrels make the most noise." She seeks to please those with whom she converses, and lo! she wearies and fatigues them. "If babblers suffered as much as they make others suffer," says one of the ancients, "they would soon be cured of their excessive desire to speak."

*

*   *

My daughters, here is a just duty which is

incumbent upon you. You must keep a severe guard over your conversation. Now your principle aim, I take it, is not to have yourselves reputed as persons of fine style and agreeable intercourse. You are Christians, hence you regard the opinion of God a thousand times more than that of the world. Therefore, you will pay more attention to arguments of the supernatural order, than to worldly arguments.

I conjure you to exercise a severe vigilance over your words, because, according to the teaching of Holy Scripture, sin is always accompanied by an unbridled loquacity and useless babbling. My daughters, you know from experience that all conversation in which you have not guarded the tongue, was a source of remorse to you. You know well that from such and such a visit, during which you have yielded to your excessive desire to gossip, you have come away with a troubled conscience. The question arose in your mind and demanded an answer: "Was the fault that I committed grave?" Now this question did not always proceed from an exaggerated delicacy of conscience.

It was the expression of a well-founded fear of having fallen into mortal sin.

Be on your guard, my daughters! You are on dangerous ground when you give expression to every thought that passes through your mind. You must take counsel from God, and say to Him: "Have I the right to say this?" If you are not extremely watchful you will fall before you know it, and unwittingly exceed the limit which separates venial from mortal sin.

Let me give you the teaching of Catholic theology on this matter: Every slander is grave when it is of such a nature as to cause serious injury to your neighbor's reputation. It is not necessary to know the gravity of the slander by searching out what damage it has actually caused to your neighbor. It is sufficient to ask yourself this question: "Was this slander of such a nature as to injure my neighbor?" If it was not, there is a venial sin, if it was, the sin is mortal.

To know why this teaching of Catholic theology is so severe, let us invert the order. Suppose you have been slandered. Oh! then what a clamor you make. All vengeance, divine and human united cannot weigh too heavily upon the impudent wretch who has dared to sully your reputation. Judge then the value that your neighbor attaches to her reputation and conclude that God is right in becoming the defender of the absent against the wickedness of the slanderer.

*

*   *

It is useless to affirm to yourselves or your friends, with your eyes raised towards Heaven, that you have the purest of intentions. This fashion of stabbing your neighbor, for the greater glory of God, is disgusting. It cannot be too deeply branded. I know of no more repugnant spectacle than that of a person who makes a profession of piety, and then tears her neighbor's reputation to pieces. But how shall we brand the act of that person who communicates frequently, and who, in a gathering of friends, becomes the echo of malevolent words which do injury to some good work, or taint the reputation of some cleric. "Oh my dear, I do not believe a word of it myself, but this is what some one said about Father so and so." But are you, who repeat these remarks, aware that in thus converting these slanderous words into one stream, you become the echo of the slander of others? I judge your action very severely, and I tremble when I find you piously posing before the Holy Table on the next morning.

"When a doctor visits a sick man," says a certain moralist, "he asks to see his tongue. That organ gives him a certain indication as to the general health of the sick man. So, from a spiritual point of view, we can tell the condition of the soul by the tongue."

My daughters, if you abandon yourselves to all the intemperances of the tongue, it is a positive sign that your souls are spiritually ill. If, on the contrary, you keep a strict watch over the tongue and prevent its excesses, rejoice: your soul is spirtually healthy. Learn to judge yourselves by this rule. Generously sacrifice for God's sake, every word however trivial it may be, which might offend against the virtue of charity, or cause injury to your neighbor.

*

*   *

The homes of many who pretend to be Christians are often schools of slander, mockery and disparagement. If an unbeliever were to assist at a repast in one of these families pretending to Christian etiquette, and reputed to be practical Catholics, he would be astonished to find malignity where he looked for the full blossom of charity, that chosen flower of the Master. What a responsibility hangs over those mothers who tolerate these detestable practices, and who, instead of holding up a high ideal to their children, let them wallow in vulgar gossip, and even encourage them in their deplorable propensity to criticize and defame every one and everything.

I conjure you, my daughters, to preserve a strict watch over your tongues, and never to pronounce before your children one single word that is contrary to charity. Then only will you have the right to preach the horror of scandal to them.   Moreover, in this matter, your example is the only preaching needed. You are the model for all the members of your family.   Let this sentiment of your responsibility, stimulate you to reject from your conversation, all rash judgments, and every habit of criticism which your children might adopt unknown to you.

St. Augustine had these words posted in his refectory: "Speak not ill of the absent." This motto proved that he was not only a saint but also a man of honor.   My daughters, you will do well to post up this motto in your homes, at least in practise   You yourselves should see that your family lives up to it.   Your voice, with a sweet firmness, should remind those who are prone to forget, that with you, and before you, no evil must be spoken of the absent.

CHAPTER X

This chapter is addressed to those whose ambition it is to avoid not only venial sin committed with deliberate intent, but all imperfection.

The meaning of certain words in our language stands out clearer when they are more clearly defined. The word *imperfection* is of these. Many persons undertake to combat all their imperfections who have only a vague idea as to just what an imperfection really is. I desire to aid my readers to form a correct notion of spiritual imperfection, which will enable them to use this word in its true sense.

*

* *

First of all, let us take care not to confound imperfection with sin. This confusion of terms is very often made in ordinary conversation.

167

Of a light slander, or a trivial lie, it is said: "This is only an imperfection." Now, that is not true. Each of these acts is a violation of one of God's commandments, and, therefore, a sin. The triviality of the violation attenuates the gravity of the fault committed, but does not change the character which classes this act in the category of sins. Therefore, we must never apply the term *imperfection* either to venial sin or the habit of this sin, however trivial the sin itself may be.

Here then is a first conclusion: *Imperfection can exist only in a free act, an act not regulated by precept.* Now indeed we see that imperfection is clearly distinct from sin. This brings us to the most delicate part of our task, *viz.,* to determine the especial condition that taints with imperfection an act which falls under no law.

This condition is the lack of coöperation with grace. Yesterday, in passing by some poor man, I heard no interior voice pressing me to give him aid. By not giving this man an alms did I commit an imperfection? Not at all!

Since I was not solicited by grace, I could not have been unfaithful to it. To-day, on the contrary, I feel inclined to give this same man an alms. Now if I refuse to perform the act which grace demanded of me, I am guilty of an imperfection. If I have not given as much as grace demanded of me I must know that I am guilty of imperfection in the measure in which I have been unwilling to respond to the divine appeal.

We have now, it seems to me, the elements sufficient to formulate a good definition of imperfection. We can call it *a partial or a total lack of coöperation with grace in a free act.* But does this definition solve all the problems which may arise in actual life? No, certainly not. But, for the present, we have an adequate idea of the word *imperfection,* and it is no longer to be feared that in theory, at least, we will create any serious confusion. The line that separates imperfection from sin is so easy to trace, that we can follow it without the least effort when a hypothetical case is in question. On the other hand, when the case is concrete, and takes on the appearance of a case of conscience which has to be settled, our task is not so simple.

Occasionally, it is true, there is no room for doubt. The prompting of grace has been so distinctly felt, and the resistance to it so clearly accentuated, that imperfection is evident. But very often the problem is not so simple. Difficulties well nigh inextricable present themselves. Vainly do we strive with a most scrupulous effort, to comprehend the case at hand. In vain do we force ourselves with the most admirable loyalty, to repeated and profound examinations of conscience. Even these do not always solve the case. A multitude of thoughts, sentiments, and volitions often escape us entirely. Moreover, there is a goodly number of interior acts the morality of which we cannot determine precisely, and thus we are forced to remain in a semi-obscurity.

However, it seems to me that it is not quite impossible to come to a practical decision as to whether this or that act has been tainted by imperfection. Why not apply the same rule that we use when we doubt whether we have resisted a temptation to the best of our ability. How do we dispel a doubt in this case? By remembering that we are not habitually disposed to offend God by mortal sin. This remembrance suffices to restore peace to our souls. Why not make use of a like remembrance to settle the uncertainty in a case of imperfection? If we are habitually disposed to follow the inspirations of grace, have we not the right to decide the doubtful case in our own favor?

Conceived under the form which I have described, imperfection becomes something realitive. Something may be an imperfection for me, but not for you, because I may have been prompted by grace, and you may not. Because of my failure to perform the act which grace demanded of me I am guilty of an imperfection, while you are guilty of no imperfection by not performing the same act. There was no question of coöperation on your part, because you were not prompted by grace. Doubtless this explains why theologians and ascetic writers, in treating of imperfection, assume a reserve which seems almost excessive. As they are profuse with details when it is a question of cataloguing sins, so they are cautious when cataloguing imperfections.

*

*   *

I foresee a difficulty which is springing up in your minds, my daughters. You are saying to yourselves: "According to the teaching of St. Thomas and the generality of theologians, no act can be called indifferent. Every act is either meritorious or sinful. Now an imperfect act is not a sin. Must we then number it among the meritorious acts?"

Assuredly, I answer. An act, although it be imperfect, can possess a certain merit.

Let us take, for example, not one of those intricate cases of conscience which serve to display the subtlety of the casuists, but a very ordinary case.

Suppose that after giving a few pennies to some poor man, I feel grace prompting me to give five pennies more. After taking thought, I decide to give him only three. Evidently there has been a resistance to grace on my part, and therefore I have become guilty of imperfection. What will be the value of my act? The sane casuist, and my good sense, respond that this act has not been as meritorious as it might have been, and I have voluntarily deprived myself of a degree of glory in Heaven. But since I have violated no precept, I have committed no sin. The moral value of my act, despite the imperfection which taints it, has not been essentially impaired. A piece of money has value despite the tarnish that has gathered on it.

Now the advocates of the opposite opinion will make this discouraging assertion: "An act is meritorious only when it has all the perfection of which it is capable." To this I answer: In that case who could acquire merit?

*

*   *

I shall not insist on the immense advantages which will accrue from a generous coöperation with the movements of grace. "This practice, earnestly continued for three months," says Père Pergmayr, "will create an admirable change in you. Your whole interior will be transformed by it." (*Méd. sur Les Sept Dons du Saint Esprit.*)

I hear another question proposed to me by one who has resolved to coöperate with the promptings of grace:

"How," she asks, "can I distinguish the movements of grace from those of nature? Confusion is so easy. How can I know whether or not there has been a resistance to grace, and consequently an imperfection?"

Let me respond by recalling the rules laid down by the saints to aid us in distinguishing the inspirations of grace from those of nature.

1st rule: All inspirations which stimulate us to flee from evil and repress evil inclinations, bear the mark of God. This is evident. The spirit of God is a spirit of holiness. It should inspire us to suppress all evil. "I judge of the presence of the Holy Spirit," says St. Bernard, "by certain movements of the heart, which prompt me to flee from evil, and to struggle against my evil propensities."

2d rule: All those inspirations which excite us to practise one of the virtues of Jesus Christ are of divine origin. "Whenever," says St. Bernard, "you feel in your heart a salutary movement which stimulates you to mortification of the body, humility of heart, the preservation of purity, the love of your neighbor, or some other virtue, do not hesitate to believe that the Holy Spirit is acting in you."

3d rule: The spirit of God is a spirit of obedience and submission to superiors. Therefore we must distrust at once every movement which impels us to act against the judgment and will of our superiors.

4th rule: "All inspirations, all interior movements come from God, if humility precedes, accompanies, and follows them." This rule is given us by Gerson.

Let us condemn with St. Bernard, whom we should take as our guide in this matter, every interior movement which inclines us, 1. To desire to be visited by extraordinary graces and virtues, by visions, revelations and other exceptional favors. 2. To disdain the practice of those virtues suited to our state. 3. To vain glory.   4. To a scorn for our neighbor.   5. To a longing for the admiration of others.

5th rule: The spirit of God is a spirit of discretion.   "The spirit of God," says Père Dupont, "exacts from us only the practice of ordinary virtues, not those beyond our powers."

Every desire for devotions, penances, and practices which conflict with the duties of our state of life, is to be regarded with suspicion. The same must be said of all those mortifications which endanger the health, or result in a serious weakening of the body.

These are some of the rules which can aid us to distinguish the movements of grace from those of nature.   Those of my readers who desire a further development of this subject, will do well to consult the excellent work of Père Pergmayr: *Trois Pas Dans l'Amour de Dieu.*

PART THIRD

THE MEANS PAR EXCELLENCE

CHAPTER I

THE HOLY MASS

My daughters, I have now come to that part of my work which is dearest to my heart. If I succeed in instilling in you a deep love for the Eucharist, if I can induce you to enter into the most intimate relations with Jesus in the Sacred Host, then the purpose of this book will be attained. Under the guidance of the Heart of Jesus you will soon realize the ideal of the truly Christian woman.

*

* *

First, let me say a few words concerning assistance at mass every day, or several times a week. Is this practice familiar to all mothers without exception? No! There are some obliged to remain at home, on account of their household duties, or the care of their children. Many mothers would like to make a truce every

179

morning with their accustomed duties, and come for a half hour to the church; but they cannot.   Many mothers heartily regret that they are bound to this or that duty, since it renders them unable to assist at mass.   I know some pious mothers who unite their intentions with those of the priest; and for want of sacramental Communion, they make a spiritual communion. Surely, God takes their good will into consideration.   The pain they experience because of their inability to assist at mass, since they offer it up to God, brings them very precious graces.   It would be a great injustice to number these mothers among the lukewarm.   But are there not some mothers who, by making a little sacrifice, could assist at mass every day, or at least several times a week?   Yes, if they would rise a little earlier in the morning, they could easily do so.   Now I am not demanding heroism.   I plead the cause of your dignity, mothers of families, and I ask you not to be so great a slave to laziness as to refuse to sacrifice one hour of sleep a few mornings in the week.

I put little faith in those headaches which you sometimes advance as an excuse. Is it not strange you are always suffering from a headache when it is a question of assisting at mass, but you never complain of a headache when it is a question of some pleasure or self-indulgence?

Still less do I accept the lack of time as an excuse, for I dare to affirm that in assisting at mass you gain time. You place in the soul a principle of order and energy, the beneficent influence of which pervades the entire day. You will work better and produce more fruit. That half hour which you give to God each morning, far from being time lost, will be the time best employed during the day. It will incite you to renounce useless reading, it will stimulate you to refrain from gossiping, and help you to cut short your purely conventional visits.

How happy I should be did these words of mine make my readers resolve to assist at mass occasionally during the week. No lukewarmness can exist under this regime, more especially if one assists at mass in the way that I shall now explain.

*

*   *

My daughters, these words are addressed to you all, whether it is your privilege to hear mass daily or only on Sundays.   Let me say to every one of you, that you must draw from this sacred act the fruit which God intends.   You must make this act a defense against lukewarmness, or a remedy for it.   Therefore, your first care should be to avoid routine.   Now to do this, you must awaken your faith when you assist at the Holy Sacrifice.   When you enter the church you should ask yourselves, what is the Catholic doctrine concerning the mass.   You should have a ready response to these questions: "Why have I come to church?"   "What value has this action which is about to be performed before my eyes?"

Will your prayer-book answer these questions?   I think not!   These prayers which you have been reading for years, and can almost recite from memory, will not, to my mind, assist you in any great degree. I fear that they have become mere words which you recite mechanically, while your eyes wander about, observing the dress and appearance of your neighbor. I would advise you to begin by making a vigorous appeal to your faith. I would advise you to reflect quietly on the grandeur of the Holy mass and on the love of that God who comes down on the altar to renew the sacrifice of Calvary.

How comes it that this advice, which entails no very great labor, finds many of you reluctant to accept it? Why do you insist on using your prayer-book, since it conveys but very little to the mind, and nothing to the heart? Alas! this question is very easy to answer. The state of lukewarmness in which you live, has made all personal reflection on the things of God extremely painful. You have a marked repugnance for the slightest productive effort, and so your laziness inclines you to adopt some kind of reading wherein the mind is free from every effort.

*
* *

Am I advising my readers not to use any book during mass? No indeed! All I ask is, that, on arriving at church, you make a few moments' reflection without the aid of a book. You might then open a book treating of the Eucharist, and, having read a few lines, close it and meditate on what you have read. This alternate meditation and reading is not at all fatiguing. It imposes only a mediocre effort on the mind, and I know that this method is within the reach of all.

I have stated that before opening your book, you must reflect. Now on what should you especially reflect? You should reflect especially on the grandeur of the act which is about to be performed. You must ponder the Catholic doctrine concerning the Holy Sacrifice, and recall to mind the sublime Reality hidden under these sacred rites, so simple in appearance. The Reality, the One whose presence your faith should affirm, is Jesus Christ. Do you remember how Jesus appeared to His Apostles gathered together in the Cenacle? Suddenly, without any exterior noise, the doors and windows being shut, Jesus stood in the midst of them. In this same manner Jesus descends upon the altar. No exterior sign betrays His presence. No apparent change is produced on the patin, or in the chalice. If you consult only your senses, they will tell you that there is nothing save a small piece of bread on the patin, and a few drops of wine in the chalice. Your faith tells you of the Real Presence of Jesus. It tells you what the mass really is, and affirms that it is the act by which Jesus descends anew and becomes as really present on the altar as He is in Heaven.

You see what appeasement this act of faith will immediately produce in your soul, and what facility it will give you in meditating. You will be possessed by this one great thought: "I am going to meet my God! Jesus is coming to me!"

What I have advised is very simple indeed, so simple that it may seem superfluous. This is not the case, however; for if you look back over the past, you will be forced to confess that you have frequently assisted at mass without making a single act of faith, or reminding yourselves, even in a vague way, of the real presence of Jesus on the altar. A sterile piety, a piety entirely superficial, is that which is not founded on the great dogma of the Real Presence.

*

*   *

Finally, you should propose to yourselves this question: "Why does Jesus descend upon the altar?" Your faith should answer: Jesus descends upon the altar to renew the sacrifice of the cross. Your faith must teach you that after the consecration, the Gentle Victim of Calvary is present before you under the Eucharistic species. Imagine you can see the wounds which furrowed that Sacred Body, and the bloody marks made by the scourge. It is that same Jesus on the altar, who pleaded with His Father for the salvation of humanity as He hung on the Cross.

Perhaps you will ask how Jesus, glorious and impossible as He is to-day, can offer Himself daily as a victim. Perhaps you will inquire what Jesus can sacrifice in the mass. Let me tell you. On the altar, Jesus sacrifices the glory with which He has been clothed since His ascension. Make a comparison between Jesus on the altar, and Jesus in Heaven. In Heaven, He is glorious and resplendent with light, a joy to the angels and the saints. Regard Him on the altar, hidden in the host. Who could recognize, under these frail species of bread and wine, the Lord who dwells in Heaven? Can you understand now, in some measure, how Jesus offers Himself as a victim, and what He sacrifices in the mass?

Moreover, I venture to say that in His eucharistic state, Jesus is more humiliated than He was on Calvary. While He was nailed to the cross, life was apparent in Him from His words, and from that great cry before He gave up the ghost. On the altar there is not the least semblance of life. Nothing, save our faith, tells us of the Real Presence of Jesus. A veil is stretched between the Victim and us, shutting us out from the sights of His immolation. Yes, on the altar, more than on Calvary, is our God humiliated.

Can you, my daughters, remain indifferent before this stupendous testimony of love? Will you not make some return to Jesus? How can you help loving a God who has loved you so much, that He suffered Himself to die on a cross for you? How can you help loving a God who immolates Himself daily for you on the altar?

My daughters, what may we not expect from the boundless love of Jesus? Had we been living in the time of Jesus, and met Him on one of His journeys through Judea, with what confidence should we have made known to Him our necessities. Our spiritual needs, our temporal needs, the needs of those we love, all these we should have exposed to Jesus with the certitude that He would grant all we asked. Is Jesus less powerful on the altar than He was in Judea? Is His arm shortened? Is He not the God whom nature obeys? Is He not the All-powerful, and the Source of all miracles?

It sometimes happens that you find the mass too long: you do not know what to say to our Lord while He is on the altar. Let me propose to you an inexhaustible subject for conversation. Expose to Jesus whatever you desire as mothers. Tell Him your trials, your fears, and your hopes. Ask Him the solution of all those difficulties which so often perplex you. If Jesus reproaches you, it will never be because you have asked too much, but rather because you have failed to be discreet in your petitions. A mass during which you would not cease to cry out your miseries to Jesus, would be a mass well heard, provided that you were not less solicitous for spiritual favors than for those of the temporal order.

CHAPTER II

My daughters, if you are tainted by lukewarmness, if you feel cold in your relations with Jesus, you should do what you instinctively do when you are physically cold. You should go near a fire. Now the fire which your souls need, really exists. It is the fire of the Sacred Heart of Jesus. By receiving the Sacred Heart of Jesus in Communion, you will soon be cured of your lukewarmness. Jesus is then in you. His heart beats near your heart, it becomes one with yours: His life is infused into your life. Between His heart and yours there is an ineffable union, and a delicious embrace, from which you will go forth seeking sacrifice and mortification for His sake.

Holy Communion is not the only means by which you can meet Jesus, and warm your heart by contact with His. Even without communicating, you can draw near this fire whenever you please. Even without placing this fire within you, you can feel its warmth. How can we do this, you ask? By making a visit to the Blessed Sacrament.

A visit to the Blessed Sacrament is like the visit of one friend to another. It is a heart-to-heart talk with Jesus.

My daughters, I know that many of you have not the time to make a visit to the Blessed Sacrament every day. But is there one among you who will tell me that she cannot spare a few moments for this visit once a week? Occasionally you will find yourselves in the vicinity of some church. Can you not pause for a moment and salute your God in the tabernacle?

*
* *

How much time should be devoted to this visit? Well, if I were dealing with a lukewarm woman, I should advise her not to devote a very long time to this heart-to-heart talk with God. A few minutes will suffice. I should not advise

her to prolong her visit to such an extent that
she will become fatigued. Become fatigued?
What am I saying? Can any one become fatigued in a heart-to-heart talk with Jesus? Is
it possible? Alas! it is. You know it from experience, my daughters. Your actual lukewarmness must be taken into account. But I
hope that after a while, the few moments which
you grudgingly give to Jesus will be lengthened
to a quarter of an hour. But, for the present,
you are only convalescent. Therefore I must
not advise food that is too heavy for your spiritual organism to digest.

On entering the church make an act of faith
in the Real Presence. To my mind, the best
way to awaken your faith from its torpor is to
picture to yourselves our Divine Lord showing
you His Heart, stretching out His arms to you,
and saying to you, as He said to the Blessed
Margaret Mary: "Behold the Heart that has
loved men so much."

Why remain in the back of the church, or hide
behind a pillar? Come near, come very near to

the Heart of Jesus; this will show our Lord that you desire to be intimately united with Him.

*

* *

Good sense, as I have said, should regulate the length of your visits. It should also regulate the method which you use in making it. To be sure, it would be ideal to use no method. A friend never prepares his words when he speaks to a friend. His heart speaks, and the expression of his face reveals his joy at being with his friend. However, I believe that this course of action is not suited to you. I doubt if it succeeds with very many.

Here is a short method which I trust will be useful to the fervent and the lukewarm alike.

On repairing to the church, try to realize the grandeur of the act which you are about to perform. When you have entered into the church, make a strong appeal to your faith, and hasten to approach near to the tabernacle, where your God awaits you with outstretched arms, and a heart overflowing with love. Let your genuflection be a true act of faith in the Real Presence.

Your visit to the Blessed Sacrament will be much more fruitful, if your union with Jesus is entire.

Now, as you know, Jesus continues in the tabernacle His immolation of the cross. His eucharistic life is an incessant repetition of the acts which He offered to His Father on Calvary: adoration, thanksgiving, petitions for pardon and for grace. Each one of these acts should have its place in your visit to the Blessed Sacrament.

1st. Adoration. The Heart of Jesus adores in the tabernacle. It is before the Divine Majesty in the attitude of absolute humiliation. How worthy of God is this homage which comes to Him from the Heart of His Son! How imperfect is our adoration when it is not united with that of Jesus! Therefore, mingle your act of adoration with the adoration of Jesus. Then adore Jesus Himself, and ask Him to strengthen your faith in His Divinity and in the Real Presence.

2nd. Thanksgiving.   You have a well founded fear of being unable to thank God worthily for all IIis benefits.   What great consolation there is in remembering that the Heart of Jesus thanks His Father for you.   Call to mind some of the favors which God has bestowed upon you, and tell Jesus how much you desire to return thanks.   You must also acquit yourselves of the immense debt which you owe to Jesus Himself. Thank Him for every action of IIis mortal life, and especially for the frightful sufferings which IIe endured for you.   Thank IIim also for the familiarity which He accords you with the Sacrament of His love.

3rd. Petitions for pardon.   In IIis tabernacle, Jesus pleads our cause unceasingly before His Father, and to appease IIis wrath, IIe shows His wounds, and reminds Him of the blood He has shed for us.   Unite your weak reparations with the infinitely efficacious reparations of Jesus. Unite with IIim in asking pardon from the Father for all the sins that have ever been committed.   You must also demand pardon from Jesus Himself.   You have so little appreciated

all that He has done for you. You have communicated with so much routine, and mingled
much indifference in all your relations with
Jesus. Hide in His Divine Heart all your negligences, and all your abuses of grace.

4th. Demands for grace. You have no need
of being guided in this last part of your conversation with Jesus. Simply tell Him in detail all your needs, temporal and spiritual. Tell
Him all that you expect from His boundless love,
and let your petitions be accompanied by that
faith which characterized the sick men in the
Gospel. The more you ask, the more you will
receive. Ask the Sacred Heart for light, and
for a tender love of the Eucharist. Moreover,
tell Jesus the needs of all who are dear to you.
Make a particular request for the Church and
for your country.

Do not retire without asking Jesus to bless
you, and while you are bowing down under His
outstretched hand, tell Him of your resolution
to guard the fruits of your visit with a jealous
care.

CHAPTER III

HOLY COMMUNION

WHEN we say that Pope Pius X is a passionate lover of the Eucharist, we announce a truth that is self-evident. His pontificate marks a celebrated date in the history of the Eucharist, and you cannot sufficiently thank God for having brought you into life in an epoch wherein the last barriers of rigorism fall, one after another, under the powerful hand of this great Pontiff.

My daughters, are you all familiar with the Decree on Frequent Communion? This decree marked a new era in the Church, and verified the prognostication of a great preacher, who some years ago affirmed that the twentieth century would be the century of the Eucharist and the Sacred Heart.

*

*   *

I do not believe I am exaggerating when I say

that this decree has created a resolution in the practice of Communion. To prove my words, I need but briefly recall to your minds the rules that have been in vogue up to this time in regard to the frequency of Communion. Theologians showed themselves very broad when it was a question of communicating once a week, but they became cautious when it was a question of communicating more frequently. They said to the lukewarm, living in the habit of venial sin, and making no effort to break this habit: "You have the right to communicate once a week, despite your lukewarmness." But when these same people expressed a desire to communicate more frequently, they prevented them, saying with St. Alphonsus: "You must earn the right to communicate more frequently by a more generous practice of virtue. As long as you have not broken away from lukewarmness, and as long as you nourish an affection for venial sin, you cannot communicate more than once a week. It would be more harmful for you than beneficial."

When, interpreting the words of St. Alphonsus, we affirmed that weekly Communion should be permitted to every one in the state of grace; when we invited all Christians without exception, the lukewarm and the fervent alike, to communicate every week, the epithet of laxists was hurled at our heads. We were reproached for too great indulgence by thus sending forth universal invitation to weekly Communion. It was feared that the respect due to the Sacrament would be in some degree lost. But it seems that we had not been indulgent enough, and that we did not have an adequate idea of the love of the Heart of Jesus. For behold how Rome has extended the privilege of frequent, and even daily Communion, to those from whom it was formerly withheld. I entreat you to weigh well these words, my daughters:

"The Church has made no precept requiring for daily Communion dispositions more perfect than those required for weekly or monthly Communion," and, "much more abounding fruit will result from daily Communion than from weekly or monthly Communion."

Thus, those among you who, up to this time,

have communicated only once a month, **may,**
nay should henceforth communicate several
times a week, if they so desire, provided these
more numerous Communions be not an impedi-
ment to the duties of their state. Let us read
the decree a little further:

"Frequent Communion, being ardently desired by our Lord and by the Church, ought to
be accessible to all the faithful, of whatever class
or condition they may be: so that no one in
the state of grace, and with the right intention,
should be turned away from the Holy Table."

The author of the decree foresaw that the
champions of the ancient discipline would come
forward with an argument on the respect due to
the Sacrament, and the irreverence that would
be shown by the lukewarm who yet cherished
an affection for venial sin. To these too zealous
defenders of the rights of God, he seemed to
say: "Be calm! Lukewarmness cannot exist
long where the practice of frequent Communion is adopted. Frequent Communion will kill
all affection for venial sin in a short time, for,
as we read in the decree: It is impossible, by

communicating every day, not to be freed little by little from venial sin, and the affection for it."

Therefore, the Pope has strongly insisted on frequent Communion as an unfailing means of ridding ourselves of venial sin. Up to this time we have waited to be delivered from venial sin, in order to be permitted to communicate frequently. Now, according to the Sovereign Pontiff, it is frequent Communion that will deliver us from venial sin. Consequently, frequent Communion is the means *par excellence* of spiritual progress. To be sure, we must be on our guard against personal interference, and submit to the advice of our confessor.

＊

＊　＊

My daughters, do you all understand, then, that the only essential for frequent Communion is the state of grace? Yes or no, are you in the state of grace? If you are, you may approach the Holy Table without fear. By the very fact that the Eucharist finds grace in the soul, that is to say, life, it acts on the spiritual organism.

It nourishes, strengthens, and increases its vitality.

Therefore, my daughters, an unfruitful Communion is impossible. An unfruitful Communion! Here again is one of those spectres which Jansenism placed before our eyes in former times. In order to deter us from approaching the Holy Table frequently, the Jansenists said: "Take care! If you do not realize such and such conditions of fervor, your Communion is unfruitful. Beware of an abuse of grace!" This is false! There is no abuse of grace, because a Communion is either good, or a sacrilege. If it is not a sacrilege, then it must of necessity be good and produce fruit.

*

* *

My daughters, when we have brought to light the doctrine of the Church concerning frequent Communion, we have not immediately won our cause. We have not carried the works of the enemy at the first onset, even though we are reenforced by the authority of the Sovereign Pontiff. Jansenism has a tough life. He who declines the invitation of the Church, takes refuge behind the respect that is due to the Sacrament, and says: "Let others profit, if they wish, by this favor granted by the Sovereign Pontiff. As for me, I fear to be familiar with our Lord in so irreverent a manner. I prefer to communicate less often, so as to communicate with more respect."

Let us see just what this objection is worth. Is it true that frequent Communion engenders an excessive familiarity with the Holy Eucharist, and a lack of respect for it? No! The contrary is true. The best way to communicate well is to communicate often, very often indeed. "You will do well," says St. Francis de Sales, "only what you do often, and the best workmen are those who ply their trade most."

Let us draw a comparison between the Communion we make at Easter or on the principal festivals, and those which we make weekly. We shall see that the words of St. Francis are true. We shall find that those who communicate most often, are those who communicate with the most respect. Because a woman who never approaches the Holy Table except at Easter, experiences a holy emotion during the days which immediately precede her Communion, because she is seized with a nervous trembling when she communicates, must we conclude that hers is a respect which is very dear to our Lord? I think not! My idea of a proper respect is the avoidance of everything that might offend Jesus. Now it seems to me, that, according to this idea, there is no better school in which to learn this respect, than the school of frequent Communion.

I have not overmuch confidence in the efficacy of the fear inspired by Communion. I do not believe that it contributes a great deal to the reform of one's life; and I surmise that those who are most agitated by vain fears when communicating, are, in fact, the most ungrateful for the benefit received, and the most prompt to forget it. If I had to choose between the excess of fear and the excess of confidence, I should not hesitate to say with St. Thomas: "In the sentiments which the Eucharist inspires, fear, doubtless, mingles with love; but a confident love is far more preferable than fear, and it is this love that the Eucharist tends to kindle in our hearts.''

Now the best way to instil a proper respect for the Holy Eucharist in our hearts is to communicate often. This is evident. An increase of love means an increase of respect, and I know of no better means for increasing that love, than frequent Communion. Experience proves that the less often we communicate, the less we are prepared to communicate. On the contrary, the more frequent our Communions, the more fruitful they are.

Some one, of course, will now come forth with certain objections. We shall answer only one of them: the objection of familiarity.

To begin with, there is a familiarity which must be avoided, and a familiarity which must be cultivated.

''If by familiarity,'' writes Mgr. De Segur, ''you mean negligence and routine, you are perfectly right. But if you mean intimacy, habitual union, and a tender and confident relinguishing of self to God, then you do very wrong to close your heart to this truly Christian familiarity.''

Who had a more profound respect for our Lord than the Saints? But did they not all love Him with the most intimate and familiar tenderness? And, aside from them, who, among the pious people that you know, have the deepest respect for God, His law, and His sacraments? Is it not those who practice their religion assiduously?

Do not fear to grow familiar with Jesus Christ, and to acquire the habit of receiving Him frequently in the Sacrament of His love. Indeed, you should make every effort to form this holy habit in yourselves. It is right to say that a woman is a true and a solid Christian, only when the service of God has become a habit to her,—second nature. Now Holy Communion is the dynamic force in this divine service. Therefore, acquire the habit of communicating well, and to accomplish this end, communicate frequently.

These few explanations will suffice, I trust, to calm the fears of those who hesitate to communicate frequently. The fear of routine is a scruple which must vanish before the formal teaching of the Church.

*

* *

In closing this chapter permit me to dispel the mistaken idea of those who imagine that they must be seriously ill to communicate at home. The result of this mistaken idea is, that when these people are confined to their rooms by sickness, they permit weeks and weeks to pass without receiving Communion. This is a very bad practice! Ask your priest to bring you holy Communion from time to time, because by yielding to the mistaken idea just mentioned, you lose many precious graces.

CHAPTER IV

COMMUNION OF CHILDREN AND YOUNG PEOPLE

My daughters, the commentary which I have just written on the decree relative to frequent Communion, would be incomplete did I not tell you the mind of the Pope concerning the Communion of children and young people. Indeed, no one has been forgotten in this decree. It is the wish of the Pontiff to apply it to all the faithful. We read in one part of this decree: "The practice of frequent Communion should be established in every college and academy." Therefore, your sons and daughters are also invited to become familiar with the Holy Table.

I shall leave your daughters aside. I shall devote myself to your sons, who do not seem pious enough, as you say, to benefit by this decree of the Pope. You will readily grant that they should communicate frequently in their earlier years, but you think that frequent Communion is incompatible with the life they lead in the world.

Upon a careful examination it will be discovered that a great deal of human respect is hidden under this conventional phraseology. It is feared, that by communicating daily, a child may be laughed at, and looked upon with contempt by the world—the world which has an indulgent smile for the most culpable crimes, but which reserves all its severity for those who strive to do their duty.

Would your prejudice vanish if I were to tell you that your sons can remain pure only by communicating frequently? Now believe those who have consecrated their lives to the direction of young people, when they tell you, that, from his twelfth to his sixteenth year, the boy has need of communicating very frequently. Why? Because this is the time when his passions awaken. Now if his will is not strengthened by frequent Communion, what hope is there that he will pass through this crisis unharmed, and preserve his innocence? Who does not know the fascination that impurity exerts over young people, whose senses are open to all impressions, and in whose heart there is a yearning to love and be loved? Oh! do not refuse your children the only weapon with which they can successfully combat their awakening passions. Do not refuse them the privilege of communicating frequently, which practise alone will keep them chaste.

Let us read the words of Mgr. Segur, a writer whose competency no one will dare to question:

"Do you desire to be chaste? Do you wish to augment the celestial treasure of holy purity in your soul? Then communicate often. The grace that comes to us in Communion is especially the grace of purity and innocence. The immaculate flesh of Jesus Christ in uniting with ours, tempers our evil inclinations. It is like water thrown on a fire. . . .

"Very frequent Communion is the salvation of all students. There are many of them, thanks to God, who, placing their conscience above pleasure, live with purity in the midst of corrupt youths, and seek, in the Sacrament of their Saviour, Jesus Christ, the strength to rule their passions, and to preserve intact the precious treasure of holy purity. Thus they go on in life worthy of their Creator, and worthy of their mothers."

To be astonished at these words is to admit that we do not know the temptations of the young man, nor the efficacy of the Holy Eucharist.   Remember the words of the Scripture in regard to the companions of Daniel who were thrown into the fiery furnace: "But the angel of the Lord went down with Azarias and his companions into the furnace: and he drove the flame of the fire out of the furnace, and made the midst of the furnace like the blowing of a wind bringing dew: and the fire touched them not at all, nor troubled them, nor did them any harm."

My daughters, within the young man there is a furnace of passion, but under the action of God in Holy Communion, the flames of impurity are either extinguished, or rendered innocuous.

As to the child whom impure vice has already seized, and who must be snatched from the tyranny of this evil, it is nonsense to imagine that any other remedy but that of frequent Communion will cure him. To prevent him from approaching the Holy Table frequently, is to condemn him to wallow in his vice without the hope of ever being freed from it. Show me one child, only one, whom abstention from frequent Communion has ever cured of vice. I pledge my word that there are many, very many indeed, for whom frequent Communion has been a cure and salvation. This is a fact, not an empty boast, and from my own experience as a priest I can prove it.

An illustrious university professor recently applied the word *failure* to a certain science. It will seem to you, my daughters, as it seems to me, that this word ought also to be applied to all education in which the science of the Eucharist has not the place of honor. The treasures which you expend in educating your sons will be wasted, if your own lives and theirs are not made fruitful by the frequent reception of Jesus, in the Sacrament of His love.

CHAPTER V

THE COMMUNION OF LITTLE CHILDREN

My daughters, I must now remind you of the decree which concerns the Communion of little children, because it has made several important duties incumbent upon you.

This decree was heartily welcomed by all priests. When we were students in theology, we were taught that the child, as well as the adult, is bound by the precept of Communion, and that when he has attained the age of reason, he cannot exempt himself from this precept without grave sin. When we raised the objection that first Communion was not made until the age of eleven or twelve, the professor either stammered out a bad excuse, or said without any hesitancy: "This is a crying abuse. When the child has attained the age of reason, he can and ought to communicate."

It is a bad practise to live just on the margin

of one of the laws of the Church. We have witnessed this in France to our sorrow. For more than a century we have postponed the religious education of the child until after his first Communion. For more than a century, we have violated a law of the Church, which binds our children as well as ourselves. We have imagined that when the child had attained his eleventh or twelfth year, the impression of his first Communion would be more profound, and the effects of that Communion more efficacious. Now all our human calculations have been baffled, and we see that we have been entirely wrong.

You understand, then, why, in the face of such results, we yearned for a vigorous hand which would lead us back into the true path. Thanks be to God it came. The Pope, be assured, has measured the difficulties of the undertaking. He weighed all sides of the question before attacking the various prejudices raised against it. He foresaw the raillery of adversaries, as well as the astonished and scandalized air of certain good Catholics. But the fear of unpopularity had no influence on so great a character. We have the happiness of having a Pope whose sole ambition it is to establish the reign of the Eucharist; and, a stranger to the ruses of politics, he prides himself on ruling the Church as a pastor rules his parish.

＊

＊　＊

My daughters, in regard to the Communion of little children, your first duty is to aid your priests to shed light on the importance and incontestable utility of this great act of the Sovereign Pontiff.

There are some people who, in matters of religion, show a spirit of contradiction that is almost the equal of mania. If the Pope says a thing is white, they say it is black. They decide on things of the Church with more assurance than St. Anselm or St. Thomas.

If a priest has any dealings with them in business matters, they snub him in fine fashion. But in religious matters they imagine that they have a perfect right to rave, and that it is proper for the most ignorant man in the world, to rise above the Pope, and make himself an oracle.

When we are obliged to deal with these presumptuous people, whose presumption is always accompanied by insults, we should not waste time in idle arguments. We should leave these maniacs to their raving. We simply become their sport if we dispute with them. They should be treated with disdain.

But aside from those adversaries whose good faith must, to say the least, be suspected, there are others who need but to be enlightened to have their prejudices removed. These persons have a right to our benevolence, and it would be very wrong to treat them with disregard or contempt. We should simply tell them the state of the question. It seems to me that it can be summed up in these words: The Pope has made no innovation. He has simply exacted the return to a general law, which, under the influence of Jansenistic ideas, had been gradually set aside. Now for this return to a law which is most efficacious for all whom it concerns, great thanks should be given to the Sovereign Pontiff.

My daughters, I can readily understand how this decree astonished even you, who are excellent Catholics. But after mature consideration, you will perceive that you have no right to come between Christ and these children, since Christ has said: "Suffer the little ones to come unto me, and forbid them not." You have no right to say: "We are wiser than the Institution of the Holy Eucharist, and we know better than He the age at which our children should communicate." Let me remind those of you who are yet astonished by the decree of the Pope, that in the ancient discipline of the Church, children were accustomed to receive Holy Communion even before the age of reason. Our fathers in the faith thought it not strange that the soul of every little child should become the tabernacle of Jesus. Yet we are scandalized at the thought of Jesus descending into the soul of a child, when it is just being enlightened by the first rays of reason. Let us trample under foot all our Jansenistic prejudices. Let us joyfully accept, in their broadest sense, these words of the Master: "Suffer the little ones to come unto me, and forbid them not."

Of course, you will say to me: "Are we showing respect for the Eucharist when we give It to this child, who hardly knows how to distinguish It from ordinary bread?" Let me ask if you know more about the Eucharist than this child. I myself, who have devoted a part of my life to the study of this Sacrament, have come to the end of my knowledge when I say: "My God is there." Now, I think I can safely say that your knowledge of the Eucharist is not much greater than mine. Oh! yes, we can enlarge upon this subject with more or less imagination and embellish it with fine phrases, but our science, at bottom, resides in an act of faith, which a child of seven years can make as well as a doctor of theology.

I should take some interest if an objection were raised on account of the child's proneness to laziness, disobedience, and falsehood. I should answer my exacting Pharisees in these terms: "You communicate often, now tell me, if you please, how you stand in the practise of these virtues, which, you say, are wanting in the child. Let me look over the balance-sheet of your lives. I find thereon a great infidelity in the accomplishment of the duties of your state, conversations in which slander and detraction mingle affronts and injuries towards your neighbor. Ill does it become you then to be so exacting towards the child, whose will is yet weak and vacillating. You have all the faults for which you reproach him, and what is more, proud as you are, you imagine you are very virtuous. If you think you are worthy to communicate, what right have you to prevent this child from communicating, who, all things considered, is far worthier than you?"

Thus should I answer my exacting Pharisees, and I venture to say that not even one of them, after glancing over her own past life, would dare to rise and say: "You are wrong! I am worthier to communicate than the child."

Oh! can we not readily understand why the God of all purity is more pleased to dwell in the little heart of the child, than in our hearts, whose purity, to say the least, is doubtful?

"We must compare," says an excellent judge, "not the first Communion made at eleven years of age, with that made at seven, but we must compare the first Communion made at eleven, with the series of Communions, arranged in gradation, which have intervened between the two ages. Now each one of these Communions has embellished the soul of the child with a divine beauty. Without effecting any sudden change, which might resemble a miracle, all these Communions taken together, have caused a continuous progress, and a constant spiritual growth, and have developed the spiritual organism normally, just as the right kind of food develops the physical organism day by day. Therefore, when your child has reached that age at which he would formally have communicated for the first time, he will be formed and fashioned for the struggle which virtue exacts." (Henri Auffroy.)

*

*   *

My daughters, to prevent your children from communicating when they have reached the age of reason, would be to come between them and the formal ruling of the Church. In other words you would be guilty of a great fault.

Not to oppose the frequent Communion of your children is only one of your duties, the least important one. Another, and a greater duty, is to prepare them to communicate as soon as they have reached the age of reason. If you yourselves cannot prepare them, you are bound in conscience to send them to the catechism class. A father or a mother who would fail to fulfil this duty, and by whose fault the child would be deprived of Holy Communion, would be guilty of grave sin.

When your children have reached the age of seven years, you have a choice between two courses of action. You must either prepare them yourselves, or send them to the priests to be prepared. She who wills the end, wills the means. If you want your children to observe the precept of Communion, a precept which binds them as well as you, you must furnish them with the means to observe it.   Now what is the means if not the catechism class?   You need not give them the catechism used by children who are nine, ten, and eleven years old, but rather that one which is used by children seven years old.   *If, through any fault of yours, the child is not prepared to communicate at least during the Easter time, you are, before God, in the state of mortal sin.*

*

*   *

Your priests joyfully accept the duties imposed on them by this new legislation.   They spare neither their time nor their energy.   You must also do your duty, by entrusting them with your children as soon as they have attained the age of reason.   You must instill in your children, from the earliest years, the knowledge of the love of Jesus, who, from His tabernacle, repeats to all generations: "Suffer the little ones to come unto me and forbid them not, for of such is the kingdom of Heaven."

CHAPTER VI

THE EUCHARISTIC EDUCATION OF THE CHILD

ARE you deeply convinced, Christian mothers, that the duty of instilling in your children a knowledge and love of the Eucharist, is more incumbent on you than on the priest? Do you know that there is a Eucharistic Education which you should give your children? Fulfil this important duty to the best of your ability, for it is perhaps the most important of all your duties.

Here are a few practical truths which will aid you to perform your task well. At what age should this Eucharistic Education begin? At the risk of astonishing you, I reply that it ought to begin before the age of reason. No praise is too great to bestow on those mothers who lead their children to the church as soon as they know how to walk, and who, showing them the door of the Tabernacle, awaken their faith in the mystery of the Eucharist. I was once moved to tears on hearing the simple language of a mother, who said to her little child: "This is the house of Jesus. This good Jesus, who loves you so much, is behind that beautiful golden door which you see before you. Tell Jesus how much you love Him. Throw Him a kiss. Promise Him that you will be a good child so that He will be pleased."

This language is very simple, but faith and love are necessary to express it. Only truly Christian mothers can find such words in their hearts.

When your children have reached the age of reason, it becomes your duty to explain to them, in the clearest and most precise language, the Real Presence of Jesus in the Eucharist. Commence by telling them that the beauty of a church does not consist in its riches and ornaments, nor in the pomp of its exterior ceremonies, but rather in the Real Presence of Jesus, who dwells in the Tabernacle day after day, surrounded by angels, who bow down in unceasing adoration before Him.

You must next instil in your children the knowledge of the Holy Mass and of the great mystery which takes place in it. This task is not at all beyond your powers. For example, you can say to them: "The same Jesus who was born in a stable, and who died for love of you on the cross, descends from Heaven at the moment when the little bell rings, and the people around you bow down. He is as really present on the altar as He was in former days in the midst of His disciples, and as He is to-day in Heaven." Where is the child, however unintelligent he may be, who cannot comprehend this language?

But do not imagine that your task is ended when you have enlightened your children on the great mystery of the Mass. You must then inspire in them a love and a yearning for this God who descends on the altar every morning because He loves us, and wishes to be near us. This is a very fruitful mine for the piety of the Christian mother to explore.

Your children will see certain persons approaching the Holy Table during Mass. Take occasions from this spectacle to impress upon them the grandeur of the act which these persons are performing. Insist on the Real Presence of Our Lord in the Host, and draw the attention of your children to the happiness of these people. What greater honor and joy can come to any one than the possesion of God in his heart? Thus you will induce your children to desire this happiness for themselves.

*

*　　*

When your children have attained the age of reason, you must fix a certain number of necessary truths in their minds. Suggest to them those thoughts which ought to dawn in the hearts of children as naturally as a beautiful day dawns. By communicating frequently yourselves, you will set them a good example.

When your children have made their First Communion, is their Eucharist education complete? Not yet! You must follow up your work by telling them, contrary to the general opinion, that there is a day in store for them which will be even happier than the day of their

First Communion. I refer to that day on which they will communicate for the second time. Make them understand well that First Communion is not the end attained, but rather a first step towards that union with Jesus, which each Communion will make more intimate. Tell them that their love for Jesus will grow more tender in each succeeding Communion.

Christian mothers, you must engrave these principles on the minds of your children. Now to do this well, and to conform to the desire of our Lord, you yourselves must know the true doctrine of the Church concerning the frequent Communion of the children. Therefore, you must put aside your own personal ideas, or rather, you must enlarge them in the measure in which the Sovereign Pontiff wishes them to be enlarged. Consequently, you must not take into account the customs of the time when you were children. It is certain that in those days the Eucharistic Bread was given out with too much parsimony. Rome has spoken! For your children as well as for you, access to the Holy Table has been wonderfully facilitated.

Instead of being astonished at the action of the Pope, and, above all, instead of criticizing it, enter into the ideas of Pius X, and instil in your children the gratitude which they owe to Jesus who desires to descend into their little hearts daily.

Christian mothers, be convinced that your children will not pass through the crisis of life successfully, unless you make them assiduous for the Holy Table.

Now there is a preaching to which they will be a thousand times more attentive than that of words. Would you have your children communicate often? Then set them an example. Communicate frequently yourselves and the Eucharist education of your children will be complete.

*

* *

The decree of Rome on the Communion of little children encountered two reigning prejudices. The first, which has to do with the age for first Communion, has gradually disappeared. The best Catholics have conformed to the ruling of the Sovereign Pontiff in this matter. But the second prejudice, which is directed against the *frequent* Communion of little children, still exists. It has a long life, and we are not as yet delivered from it.

However, the decree has left no room for doubt or equivocation on this point. We read that "All who have the care of children ought to see to it that they approach the Holy Table often after their first Communion, and, if possible, every day, since Christ and our Holy Mother Church ardently desire it. Let care be taken that they communicate with the devotion which becomes their age."

Thus we see, my daughters, that our Lord calls these little children to His Table every day. Oh! I know all the objections which will surge up in your minds. I hear you exclaim on the rashness, as you style it, of this measure. But you must submit respectfully to the ruling of the Pope, because, as you know, he is commissioned by God to interpret the thoughts and desires of our Lord infallibly. The words of the Sovereign Pontiff may call for explanation and enlightenment, but they must always be accepted with submission.

What are the duties which the decree of 1910 has made incumbent on every Catholic mother who is solicitous for the Eucharist education of her children? I yield to Cardinal Genari an authorized commentator:

"Every day," writes this eminent prelate, "all children who have parents, guardians, or diligent and pious confessors, should approach the Holy Table. Moreover, these parents, guardians, and confessors are held to procure this result in so far as it is possible. Now if it be impossible for those who live in the midst of the world to communicate every day, they ought to communicate at least on feast days, and bring their children with them to the Holy Table. Those days when they can do this, they ought to do it, for the children are obliged to hear Mass as well as they. . . . It would be a grave fault not to take account of this precept: All those who have the care of children ought to see that they approach the Holy Table often after their first Communion, and, if possible, even every day.   These persons sin therefore: (a) parents who do not take it upon themselves to have their children communicate often, and if possible, every day; (b) confessors, who do not exhort and aid in the fulfilment of this precept; (c) educators, who show indolence or bad will in this matter; (d) pastors, who, in public and in private, do not exhort children to communicate frequently.''

*

*   *

My daughters, from what has been said, you must admit that daily Communion ought to be the normal practise of every Christian who lives in the state of grace.   Consequently it ought to be yours, Christian mothers, to whom I address these words.   You yourselves must adopt this practise under penalty of opposing the formal ruling of the Church.   Therefore, what right have you to make an exception for your children?   If you think that their hearts are purer than yours, do you not also think that the God of all purity would be pleased to dwell in them as much, if not more, than in yours?   How illogical it is, then, not to stimulate in your children a practise which will continue with them throughout their lives. Remember well that if your children do not adopt this practise in their early years, they will find a great many reasons for avoiding it when their passions are awakened.

Therefore we have the right to conclude that if daily Communion is not encouraged, *so far as possible,* when your children have attained the age of reason, it has small chance of ever becoming a habit with them when they come to maturity. I have said advisedly, *so far as possible,* for I am aware that there are certain material obstacles which can prevent the realization of this ideal. Nevertheless, you should unceasingly hold up the ideal of frequent Communion to your children. Consequently you should induce them to communicate on Sundays, and if possible also on Saturdays during the scholastic year; but you should take care to have them communicate especially during the time of vacation, when material obstacles are removed to a great extent. You should at all times encourage them to increase the number of their Communions, and thus aid them to respond to the desire of our Lord.

I should be very happy if each one of my readers were to acquire a thorough knowledge of the Eucharist program drawn up by Pius X, and to consider daily Communion as the ideal for children from the first awakening of their reason. I wish that all who can, would take to themselves these words of the venerable Cottolingo: "If we were permitted to communicate more than once a day, we ought to be only too happy to do so; but since only one Communion is permitted, I will not deprive myself of it, and I cannot consent to deprive of it, even once, a person whom I love."

CHAPTER VII

THE CHURCH

My daughters, in one and the same love you embrace Jesus Christ and the Church, and you are right. The Church is the representative of Jesus Christ. In speaking to you of your duties towards the Church, I am not deviating from my subject. I am merely amplifying the commentaries which I have made on your duties towards Jesus in the Sacred Host.

*

*   *

Your first duty is to adhere firmly to all that the Church teaches. There exists to-day a degenerate Catholicism, a Catholicism polluted by incredulity, against which every one of you without exception must be on your guard. I do not believe I am exaggerating when I say that, in our modern society, there is a multitude

234

of people who do not know how to counteract
the effects of this poison which the Sovereign
Pontiff has lately branded and condemned
under the name of *Modernism*. These people
have a strange mixture of Catholic belief and
personal independence. They make a selection
among the dogmas of the Church. They accept
those which conform to their own personal
ideas, and reject those which they do not understand, taking refuge behind a sceptical: "Who
knows?"

I do not wish to be accused of pessimism, but
I cannot help thinking that very many of these
people will experience some disagreeable surprises, when they appear before the judgment-
seat of God. They feel safe at the present time,
on account of their fidelity to all the exterior
practises which Catholicity prescribes, the
practise of frequent Communion being no exception. Indeed I know many of this type who
communicate frequently. But there is one sin
which they have omitted to accuse themselves of
in their confessions, a sin which places them in

a very bad position relative to God.   This sin is their indecision, which makes them waver between Catholic faith, and rationalistic negation. I experience sentiments of anguish when I think of these people who accept the dogmas that please them and reject those that displease them, or who vacillate between affirmation and negation in regard to one especial dogma.

*

*   *

My daughters, I entreat you to oppose in yourselves and those around you, this fashion of interpreting the authority of the Church. Teach your children that one dogma has not more certitude than another; that the edifice of Catholic truth is all of one piece; and that not one stone can be taken away without disturbing the whole building.   If they have a tendency to question the authority of the Church, confront them with these two questions: "Is Jesus Christ God?"   "Has Jesus Christ established the Church to teach infallibly in His place?" The duty of bending unquestioningly before all truth taught by the Church will be imposed on them by their response to these two questions.

*

* *

My daughters, submit with a filial docility to the commands and directions of the Church. Question neither her right to command nor the opportuneness of her commands. The church has the right to determine for herself her own field of action, and no one should dare to interfere with her, or enclose her within any fixed limits.

You must be especially docile when the Church tells you that this or that book is dangerous, and that you should not read it. Words fail me in branding the conduct of those women who pay no attention to the proscriptions of the Index, and consider it only a slight fault to read a book which the Church has condemned. I tremble when I see these women approaching the Holy Table, and when I hear them say, at a reunion of friends, a few hours afterwards: "These proscriptions of the Index are all well enough for children. We live in an age when we do not need to trouble ourselves whether the Church has condemned a book or not." Oh rash women! May these mothers who despise the most holy authority which can be relied upon here below, some day find, by a just return, their own authority questioned and despised at their very hearth-stone.

*

* *

The Church is not .only an authority commanding faith and obedience; she is also a mother who loves us and commands us to love her. Let me point out to you one especial reason for loving the Church. To-day, the Church is hated with a hatred which I do not fear to call satanic. She is the representative of God and hence she is the personification of good. It is but natural, therefore, that all who bear the seal of the Demon, should rush to the assault of so hated an enemy. The Church has been hated throughout the centuries, but in our day this hatred has attained proportions which history has never known before. Men can be found who make an open and avowed profession of insulting and calumniating this indulgent mother.

My daughters, do you not realize that in the face of so great a hatred, you have a sweet and solemn duty to perform? It is your duty to love the Church, your mother. You must love her the more because she is hated. When a blasphemy reaches your ears, you must offer up an act of love to our Lord. Make amends, by an act of homage, for every outrage directed against Holy Church. Give all the publicity possible to your profession of love for her.

"At the crucial moment, this moment for example, we cannot remain neutral," says a great orator. "We must enlist in one or the other of the two contending armies. To lean sometimes toward the Church, sometimes toward the enemies of the Church, is not only weakness but cowardice, and this cowardice cannot long continue without ending in treason or apostacy. At the crucial moment, this present moment for example, not to declare one's self is to desert; not to act is to betray."

*

*   *

My daughters, your love for the Church should also manifest itself by sacrifice. Almost all of you can give up certain pleasures and luxuries, and in this way react against your vanity, and the factitious needs which you yourselves have created.

You are right in thinking that, according to my programme, the economy realized by your abstention from these pleasures and luxuries is not so much destined to increase your wealth as to serve the needs of the Church. At the present moment you must make a more energetic effort than ever before, so that none of the essential foundation-stones of the Church may be jeopardized and that none of the indispensable wheels in her machinery may become warped or broken. This effort all of you can make, according to your means, by sacrificing a small part of your pleasures and luxuries for God and the Church.

Made in the USA
Monee, IL
07 March 2022